Archaeology is
Awesome!

Andrew Kinkella
Moorpark College

Kendall Hunt
publishing company

Cover © Shutterstock.com

Kendall Hunt
p u b l i s h i n g c o m p a n y

www.kendallhunt.com
Send all inquiries to:
4050 Westmark Drive
Dubuque, IA 52004-1840

Copyright © 2022 by Kendall Hunt Publishing Company

ISBN: 978-1-7924-9306-5

Published in the United States of America

Contents

 Contents

PART THREE
Great Themes in Archaeology

Preface

This book is an honest and fun journey into the world of archaeology. My goal is to let you experience what it is like to be an archaeologist, from the excitement of the greatest discoveries to the hardships of long months of fieldwork. Along our journey together, I will teach you the core concepts of archaeology while we experience the excitement, romance, and dedication involved in unlocking the story of our past.

I wrote this book because one of my favorite things to do is teach introductory archaeology classes, and I wanted to have a companion textbook that made you as passionate about archaeology as I am! I have found that it is easiest to learn and understand archaeology if it is broken down into three basic sections: The history of archaeology (early archaeologists and famous finds—Chapters 1–5), the doing of archaeology (the nuts and bolts of how to record an archaeological site through mapping, excavation, and lab work—Chapters 6–9), and great themes in archaeology (how things like the environment and the law affect the modern practice of archaeology—Chapters 10–15).

Most chapters are organized like this:

- First, I begin with a personal story of mine that relates to the content.
- Second, I explain the main ideas and concepts to be learned. Included in this section are a series of YouTube videos from my channel "Kinkella Teaches Archaeology" that you can access at any time to augment your learning experience. The videos will play on your smartphone by simply scanning the QR codes interspersed throughout the book. The videos are short, lighthearted, and fun. Sometimes they expand on the core concepts, sometimes they give examples, and sometimes they simply tell a funny story relating to my many adventures and experiences as a professional archaeologist.

- Third, there will be a "Thought Experiment." This will be a general question about the core concepts of the chapter that needs your special attention. When the "Thought Experiment" appears in the middle of the chapter, read it, and when you see the word "THINK" in capital letters, think! This means stop reading and take a few minutes to think about the question. When you have your own answer, then read on. I will give some possible answers at the end, but there are often many other possibilities that I have not listed that you can discuss with your professor, your fellow classmates, or even enjoy on your own.
- Lastly, there will be one or two examples of famous archaeological sites, people, or events that relate to the chapter theme.
- At the end of the book is a "Field Journal," which is a collection of hands-on exercises that relate to the "Doing Archaeology in the Field" section, such as making a map, drawing an artifact, or recording an excavation. These projects will be simple, fun activities that you can do at home or at school without the need of any special equipment. The pages are made to be torn out of the binding of the book, so you can turn in your journal to the professor when you are finished.

Interspersed throughout the book and the YouTube channel will also be friendly tips on how to survive in archaeology, whether it be on an archaeological dig or in the academic world. The examples will be my own, in my own voice, based on real experiences that I have had. Sometimes funny, sometimes serious, and always brutally honest! My pledge to you is simple: I will show you that archaeology is awesome. I will not destroy your enjoyment with horrible academic jargon or complicated examples. I will tell each story in a straightforward and fun manner. I will make sure you learn everything you need to learn to either go onward in archaeology or to just enjoy being an informed citizen. In exchange, you must be a willing student, and allow yourself to experience how archaeologists uncover what is literally the Greatest Story of Them All—the story of our shared human past.

PART ONE

The History and Romance of Archaeology

In this first third of the book, we will explore the rich history of archaeology and the famous sites that have captured the attention of the world and continue to excite and fill us with wonder.

CHAPTER 1

Hello and Welcome to Archaeology!

Stranded in the Jungle at Night

We had been walking for hours in the darkness. It was almost four o'clock in the morning, and I was exhausted. Filthy and soaking wet, I shuffled vaguely forward on heavy, mud encrusted boots. I had a bad feeling that we were walking in the wrong direction, but I didn't have the energy to worry about it anymore. The truck we had been driving had been irretrievably stuck in the mud at three o'clock the previous afternoon during a rainstorm deep in the Belizean jungle. We had spent several hours attempting to get the truck out of the mud, but after the Sun went down, our small crew of seven made a group decision to walk back to the closest village, seven miles to the south. Using a compass, a few AA-battery flashlights for light, and machetes to cut a trail, we would traverse those seven miles through the jungle in darkness.

As we walked, the choice to leave the truck was looking worse and worse. When you are lost in the wilderness, the best thing to do is stay put, as rescuers will be able to more easily find you. Continuing onward when you are lost just makes you more lost. We knew this but decided to leave because we were low on water, we weren't technically "lost" (we had a map of the area, a compass, and could vaguely figure out where we were), and there was nobody looking for us.

As the hours continued to drag on and physical exhaustion gradually took over, it became increasingly difficult to judge time and distance, and to make good decisions. In this mental haze, I started to mistrust my own compass. "Are we still really walking south? It doesn't feel like it at all." I forced myself to trust my compass, even though it felt utterly wrong. It is extremely difficult to figure out where you are in the jungle, even in the best of circumstances. You are lost in an unyielding sea of vegetation and cannot see any landmarks. As crew morale plummeted due to stress and exhaustion, our walking pace had slowed to an energy-less slog. Stronger members of the crew would backtrack to help weaker members. It got to a point where I wasn't quite sure if we were making any headway at all. Maybe we were just walking in a big circle. Our plan to walk to the village had degraded into an exhausted, confused group of people lost in the jungle in the rain at night.

Just after four in the morning, after I was sure we had been going the wrong way for quite some time but my compass said otherwise, I saw a sliver of light in the distance. It was a single, dim bulb from the village. We were saved!

This is just another typical day on an archaeology project. There are two important lessons here:

1. Always trust your compass.
2. You must always keep walking.

Archaeology is not about treasure. It is not about skeletons, or pyramids, or mummies or gold. It is about discovering the story of the past, which you will only ever uncover if you keep walking.

What is Anthropology?

In order to understand archaeology, we must first understand anthropology, which is the larger discipline of which archaeology is a part. **Anthropology** is the study of people.

I could give you a long, overly academic definition like "anthropology is the study, past and present, of human beings and their associated culture, beliefs and lifeways through time in relation to themselves and their environment" but it is much more useful to remember that anthropology can be defined with four simple words: *the study of people.* Anthropology is simply the most basic way to study human beings. An old professor of mine said "Anthropology is the study of anything human beings ever did . . . ever." Because anthropology is the most general way of studying humans, we say that anthropologists are **holistic**, which means we study people in a very broad way. All of the other disciplines that study people, such as sociology, religious studies, economics, biology, history, or psychology all do it in a more focused, narrow manner. Since we have a broader reach than any of the other disciplines, we can study more aspects of what it means to be human, and we can draw far-reaching conclusions about the human condition. This is what makes anthropology the best!

In order to study people fairly, we always try to maintain **cultural relativism** and steer away from **ethnocentrism.** Cultural relativism is the idea that we should not pass a value judgment on other cultures, that each culture is no better or worse than another. This is the most powerful idea in all of anthropology. If we forget to be culturally relative, we stop being anthropologists. Ethnocentrism is the opposite of this, the idea that one culture is better than all the others. If you think your culture is the best, you are ethnocentric. This does not mean that you cannot be patriotic. We can all be patriotic while still maintaining a culturally relativistic approach to all the other cultures on Earth. If the only thing I teach you in this entire book is to be less ethnocentric and more culturally relativistic, mission accomplished! When we add the inclusiveness of cultural relativism to the broad, holistic approach that anthropologists take when studying cultures, we call this the **anthropological perspective**. The anthropological perspective is a powerful way in which to see the world. It provides you with a lens to see the world through broad inclusivity, where you are open to different people and different ways of doing things.

The Four Fields of Anthropology

Anthropology (the study of people) is divided into four fields. They are:

Cultural Anthropology
Biological Anthropology
Linguistics
Archaeology

Each of these fields forms one quarter of the anthropological pie. As you would expect, each field focuses on one specific aspect of studying people. Note—Sometimes you will hear that anthropology has a fifth field, called "Applied Anthropology." I am not a fan of this idea. "Applied Anthropology" just means anthropology that is used in the real world (like a job working for the government, or for a nonprofit company). Each of the four fields has an "applied" aspect to them, which means that there is no reason to add an awkward "fifth field" to the original four.

Cultural anthropology is the study of living cultures.

When we say the term "anthropologist" with no qualifier, this is the type of anthropology that comes to mind. Cultural anthropologists will study a living group of people, focusing on aspects of culture such as belief systems, social organization, food, and adaptations to the environment. They will write up their research in an **ethnography**, which is a book on the culture often with chapters based on concepts like the ones I just listed. Cultural anthropologists are known for using **participant observation,** where the anthropologist lives with the group they are studying for long periods of time to immerse themselves into the culture.

Biological anthropology is the study of the human animal.

A biological anthropologist studies the basic biological aspects of humans. The three main aspects of biological anthropology that a biological anthropologist may focus in are evolution, primatology, and the human fossil record. Biological anthropology is the most scientific of the four fields, where science takes precedence over humanities (see Chapter 3 for more on this debate). You might notice this at your college, where you will receive a biological sciences credit for taking a biological anthropology class. None of the other four fields will give you a science credit (they will give you a social science/humanities credit). Fun Fact—**forensic anthropology** (the study and reconstruction of crime scenes) is an offshoot of this field.

Linguistics is the study of language.

A linguist will study the deep history of human communication, how languages grow and change, and how they interrelate. It is the smallest of the four fields.

Archaeology is the study of the human past.

Sometimes the human cultures that archaeologists study are still living today, and sometimes they have long vanished. We reconstruct what happened in the past using artifacts. I would define archaeology like this: *Archaeology is form of anthropology that uses artifacts to tell the story of the human past.* Of the other three fields, archaeology most resembles cultural anthropology. The background of both fields is very similar in terms of studying people, the only real difference is that cultural anthropology focuses on the present, whereas archaeology focuses on the past. If archaeology is done at a site of a very recent age (such as at a World War II battlefield), we refer to this as **historic archaeology**, meaning the site is from the modern era where historic records can also be consulted when recreating the past.

In archaeology, **artifacts** are of supreme importance. Artifacts are actual pieces of the past that were made by humans, like a coin from a thousand years ago, a broken piece of pottery from an ancient city, or an arrowhead that was lost during a hunt. Artifacts are sometimes called "**material culture**," meaning that they are actual physical pieces of culture (the terms "artifact" and "material culture" can be used interchangeably). Any human-made objects that you have, from your shirt to your car keys, are artifacts or "material culture" of modern society.

The greatest quality that artifacts possess is that they are real and can be used to get real data and facts about the past. This enables us to tell the story of the past using facts, not feelings. One of the best parts about archaeology is that we deal in facts, and we can prove things about the past using facts that we tease out from the artifacts. You may have intense feelings about what happened in the past, but (to put it bluntly) archaeology does not care about your feelings! You must be able to prove what you are saying about the past based on artifacts! There is a whole industry based on feelings and false claims, which produces fake stories with no facts. It is called pseudoarchaeology (think *Ancient Aliens*) which we will explore in Chapter 14.

The job of the archaeologist is to find artifacts and then use them to tell the story of the past. Sounds pretty easy, yes? There is one big problem: Time. Time is not our friend. Time makes things impossibly old, and old things fall apart and die. Time allows things to get lost and destroyed. What if you are working at an archaeological site that is a thousand years old? Think about how much time that has gone by since human beings lived there. Think about how much has been lost. I like to think of archaeology as the practice of "three pieces of the thousand-piece puzzle." You have three pieces (your artifacts) of a thousand-piece puzzle. Your job is to tell me about the image on the puzzle, using your three pieces. What can you tell me about the image? What has been lost?

It gets worse. Archaeology is not about reconstructing the past of a week ago. It is about reconstructing the past of hundreds or thousands of years ago. If we were trying to tell the story of an archaeological site that is 1,000 years old, that would be 50,000 Tuesdays ago. King Tut lived in the 1300s BC. That is 3,300 years ago, or 170,000 Tuesdays ago. Again, how much has already been lost after one week? Imagine how much is gone after 50,000 or 170,000 weeks. Isn't it incredible that we find anything at all? You see how those small bits of the past are actually very precious?

What did you do last Tuesday?

One of the best ways to understand how an archaeologist thinks is to take a moment and think about what you did seven days ago. For the sake of argument, I will explain this as if you are reading this on a Tuesday (you use the actual day you are reading this). Tell me what you did seven days ago, last Tuesday. How much do you remember from last week? There is no gold star at the end of this exercise—it only works if you are honest. Also, you cannot use your schedule to help with your memory, meaning, since you know you work on

Tuesday nights from 5–9, that does not mean you can remember last Tuesday. What I want is an exact memory from that day seven days ago. It can be big or small. See yourself in your mind's eye precisely doing something from that day. **THINK**.

If you cannot do this, don't worry. I find that most of us have no idea what we did last Tuesday (In my classes, it's usually only about 25% of people who can remember something concrete). Now realize how much of last Tuesday is gone. It has only been seven days of time that has passed, yet how much of last Tuesday is left? Five percent? How many moments and experiences are already lost? Most of them? Based on your memory of seven days ago, there seem to be very few left.

Now let's give this thought experiment some weight. Most of us can't really remember much from last Tuesday, and those who can, might remember one or two small specific moments. What if you were forced to remember what happened last Tuesday? What if there was a knock on your door right now, and it was the police. You are implicated in a murder that happened seven days ago. You must account for your whereabouts. You must *prove* where you were last Tuesday.

How do you do it? What do you use to prove where you were? You need **data** and **facts**. The police don't care about where you "think" you were, or where you "feel" you might have been. Where do you look to get data and facts to prove you didn't commit this crime? Hint—now is the time to use your work schedule. **THINK**.

List some possible data and/or facts that prove where you were:

_____   _____

_____   _____

_____   _____

As an example, your phone provides lots of information about your personal whereabouts from the last week. Your phone may have recorded GPS points of where you were last Tuesday. It may include photos of where you were last Tuesday. There may be text messages, phone calls, and social media posts that can prove where you were. Let's make it harder. What if you don't have a smart phone? You could ask friends about where you were last week. You could look at your work schedule, or bank statements. You could dig through your dirty clothes and find what you wore last Tuesday. You could even go through your trash and find what you ate last Tuesday.

All of these examples (and there are many more) are how you can get data and facts about the past of one week ago. The more you have, the better.

Who is the Archaeologist?

Who is the type of person that attempts to reconstruct the past of thousands of years ago? Who becomes an archaeologist?

We will explore archaeology as a career in the final Chapter 15 of this book. For now, we want to know that archaeology is an academic discipline, so an archaeologist is someone who must have and advanced degree and training. This advanced training will allow them to specialize in four categories of archaeological research: **Area, time, artifact,** and **skill**.

An **Area** specialty is a location on the globe that is the focus of your research. An archaeologist will often refer to themselves based on where they work, calling themselves things like an Egyptologist, a Mayanist, an Andeanist, or an Americanist.

A **Time** specialty for the archaeologist could be as simple as Prehistoric or Historic. One might study New Kingdom Egypt, Classic Period Maya, or Classical Greece and Rome. It is a specific bracket of time in the past that you know well.

An **Artifact** specialty is the general group of artifacts that an archaeologist will focus on during their studies. The Big Three are ceramics, lithics (stone), and bone.

An archaeologist will have a specialized **Skill** that they bring to the table of a working archaeology project. Common skills include advanced training in excavation methods, survey and mapping, and laboratory analysis.

To take me as an example, I am a Maya archaeologist (area) specializing in the Late Classic Period of 600–900 AD (time) with specialties in stone tool analysis (artifact) and mapping (skill). In addition, most archaeologists also have a secondary set of specialties. My secondary specialties are Southern California archaeology (area) of the Middle Period from 500 BC to 1300 AD (time). I have a useable background in ceramics (artifact) and I also have advanced training in underwater archaeology (skill).

The more skills an archaeologist possesses, the better, but we cannot do it all ourselves. Archaeology is a team sport. We are helped by many other specialists, such as geologists, photographers, geographers, anthropologists, and historians. In addition, local people, students, and volunteers provide indispensable help on archaeological projects (more on this in Chapter 6).

What Does an Archaeologist Do?

As we have already learned, an archaeologist tells the story of the past through artifacts. In order to tell the story completely, an archaeologist follows four general steps: Discover, Record, Interpret, and Protect (easily remembered as **DRIP**). Each of these steps must be completed, or any excavations that are being done are not up to ethical and professional standards.

Discover—An archaeological site is discovered on one of two ways; either it is found by accident, or it is located during a planned archaeological survey. Once the site is found, it may also be excavated to uncover artifacts hidden under the ground.

Record—After the initial discovery of the site, the site is mapped using equipment such as a compass, GPS, and a transit, and high-quality maps are constructed using the location data. Any excavations are recorded by filling out paperwork, drawing the layers of earth and artifacts as they are uncovered, taking precise measurements of depth and location, and taking lots of photos of the site, excavations, and artifacts. After the excavation is complete, the artifacts are recorded in better detail in a laboratory setting, where they are cleaned, weighted, measured, and typed. Select artifacts may also be sent out for dating, such as by Carbon-14.

Interpret—Once the artifacts have been fully recorded, they are used (along with the maps) to reconstruct the past and tell the story of history. This story will be written down in reports, articles, and books. Within the interpretation phase, there are three main aspects of the past that archaeologists try to figure out. They are **timeline, lifeways,** and **change over time**, conveniently abbreviated as **TLC**.

Timeline—If I asked you, "what is the first thing you think an archaeologist tries to figure out about an archaeology site?" you would probably say "How old it is." We try and reconstruct the timeline of the site—when people got there and how long they stayed. Dating methods like Carbon-14 are very important in answering this question, as are the style of the artifacts that you find (see Chapter 5).

Lifeways—Here we are trying to reconstruct a typical day in the life of a person that lived at the site. It is as if we are a cultural anthropologist from the time describing how people lived. What did they do with their days? What did they wear? How did they feel? What did they eat? What did they believe? As you might imagine, some of these questions are really hard to answer using artifacts!

Change over Time—As centuries and millennia roll by, the people who lived at the archaeological site where you are working must have experienced times of great change. Was there a flood one year? Did they stop hunting and gathering for food when they discovered farming? Why did they begin having a monarchy, when they did not have one before? Was there a time of devastating warfare? Famine? Some of the deepest and most perplexing questions in archaeology can be found here. If you can explain why people changed how they lived over time, it is an extremely important and satisfying part of the story of the past.

Protect/preserve—Finally, the archaeologist must assure that the archaeological site will not come to further harm from their activities. The archaeologist must backfill any open excavations, reconstruct or stabilize any structures that have been disturbed by excavation activities, and make sure to the best of their ability that the site is safe from long-term looting or destruction.

When an archaeologist begins their studies of an ancient culture, it is a journey from the **known to the unknown**. We always start at a known point. This may be the spot on the map that we know the precise location of before we head out into the jungle. This may be the surface of the ground before we begin excavations, or the surface of the ocean before we dive down to the shipwreck. This may be an archaeological site that was already recorded years ago, before we explore for ones nearby that are unknown. On a philosophical level, it may be the knowledge that other archaeologists have already recorded, that you will use as the foundation for your own research. It is important to consciously know and record your starting point, in both the physical and mental realms, so that new information can be tied to the old.

As an odd postscript to what an archaeologist does, **we destroy what we study.** What I mean here is that once an archaeological site is excavated, it cannot be either undone or redone. A human skeleton or artifact cannot be "put back" after it is excavated. You have one attempt to remove the artifact while recording everything you can about it. Once the artifact has been removed, the ability to get certain types of data vanishes. This means that you must be utterly careful and proceed smartly as you uncover the past - there are simply no second chances.

What Does an Archaeologist NOT Do?

An archaeologist does not loot. **Looting** is the unlawful stealing of archaeological artifacts and destruction of archaeological sites for personal gain. There is *never* a reasonable time to do this. Looting is the single largest destroyer of archaeological sites and artifacts. When people loot, they are destroying history. They are destroying stories from the past that will never be told. Instead of practicing "DRIP," and "TLC," they only get to "D" and ruin everything else for the rest of us. It is a selfish, disrespectful practice.

The problem with looting is philosophical as much as it is physical. People who loot are doing it for their own personal gain, whether it be for a personal collection or to make money. Either way, they are putting a value onto archaeological artifacts that they never had before. Instead of calling objects from the past "artifacts," the looting world calls them "**antiquities**." What is the difference? Think about it. "Artifacts" have no monetary value; they are simply old objects from the past. "Antiquities" have a monetary value attached. You see antiquities in auction houses where they are up for sale. "Artifacts" are worth everything and nothing at the same time. They are only worth the information that you can tease out of them to help you tell the story of the past. This is true even for something as valuable as a gold bar (see below)!

There is a terrible idea that floats around in our society called "finders keepers," which is the idea that if you find it, it is now owned by you. It is an attractive idea to many people because what it means is that you get something for nothing, but let's think about it in simple terms. If you leave your cell phone in class, and then I find it, is it now mine? No! It's still yours, you just lost it. *Finding something does not mean you own it.* Archaeologists do not own the artifacts they find, nor would they want to. The idea of ownership the past is an essential topic that we will explore more in Chapter 13. For now, remember that looting is always bad, and it destroys our shared past.

Why bother doing archaeology?

Why bother doing archaeology? Why not just let looters have it all? Why not build condominiums over archaeological sites, and forget the whole subject? More than anything, archaeology it is intrinsically interesting. We uncover history that would not otherwise be known, recover alternate ways of doing things that have been forgotten, and add real data to history through artifacts.

What makes archaeology so interesting? Ultimately, we in archaeology attempt to answer the great questions of human existence. Can an economics major claim that they are attempting to answer where we came from? Do business majors delve into what it means to be human? Actually, they do, but it is not the same.

Examples of The Big Questions that archaeology tries to answer:

Where are we from?
Who came before us?
How did we get here?
What does it mean to be human? (Who are we?)

Where did they go?

Who owns the past?

These questions are at the heart of our attempt to understand ourselves. They are what will always keep archaeology relevant in the modern world.

A Gold Bar

Treasure and archaeology have been intrinsically tied together since the beginnings of archaeology, but treasure for treasure's sake is not very interesting, and I can prove it to you. Imagine that I have a gold bar. I pull it out of my backpack and put it in front of you. Your first reaction is "Wow! That's a gold bar!" Why are you so excited by it? It is because the gold bar is known to have a very high monetary value, and chances are you have never seen one before. Now that I have set a gold bar in front of you, what do you want to do with it? You might want to joke that you want to steal it, but let's say you can't steal it. What do you want to do? You want to touch it. You want to hold it and feel its weight in your hand. You want to experience the gold bar for its gold bar-ness. After a few moments, that excitement dissipates. You have now experienced the gold bar.

Now what if I continue, and say to you five minutes later, "Hey! Check out this gold bar!" You would think I was a bit strange. You already saw the gold bar. What if I said it yet again after half an hour? In a very rapid amount of time, you become disinterested with the gold bar. You have experienced the gold bar, and there is nothing else to do with it. That is because beyond its monetary value, this gold bar has no story. Treasure for treasure's sake is BORING. If I could tell you the list of owners of the gold bar, where the gold bar was made, what banks it had been in, who stole it and who died for it, then you would be interested! The gold will catch your attention, but it is the story that keeps you interested.

Archaeology is not a search for treasure. It is a search for much deeper, more philosophical, and much more rewarding things like **identity** and **understanding**. Ultimately, archaeology is a fantastic journey to discover the elusive **story of the past**.

© Andrew Kinkella

EXAMPLE: How did I become Dr. Andrew Kinkella, archaeologist?

Who am I? Who is this person who is writing this book, whose words are being spoken in your head as you read? My journey into archaeology began in college, when I took an introduction to archaeology class my first semester of my freshman year. It was taught by an absolutely dynamic professor, who was a consummate storyteller and public speaker. While I ended up with a "B" in his class, and I was far from sure that I wanted to be an archaeologist, I learned one important thing about myself—I wanted to travel the world and have amazing experiences like that professor did!

I got my chance two years later, when another archaeology professor offered a three-month field school in Belize, Central America to work at a large Maya site in the jungle. It was an amazing, galvanizing experience. By the end of that field season,

I was hooked. I continued to go to Belize almost every summer after that, sometimes for as long as four months, sometimes for only two weeks or a month. I worked on several different archaeology projects in Belize, and I continued my education at the same time, getting a Master's degree and then finally a PhD, always returning to the Maya jungles of Belize. I was able to use other skillsets I had for my research, such as scuba diving, to study the underwater world of the Maya cenotes. In the world of archaeology (if you Google my name), I am most known for my research on the Maya cenotes of Belize.

Since I only went to Belize in the summers, I was able to sample archaeology in other parts of the world as well, working on projects in Germany, Baja Mexico, Guatemala, Arizona, and on a shipwreck in Northern California. I was also always interested in the archaeology of where I lived, and I have been privileged to work extensively on local Native American sites in Southern California. All of these experiences informed my style of practicing archaeology, and in no small measure made me the person I am today.

I have absolutely enjoyed my life in archaeology. I have been able to have experiences that most other people have not. To be able to say I am an "archaeologist" is always fun and rewarding, and I have found that it has opened many other doors for me in life that have nothing to do with archaeology. This is because a job like "archaeologist" has what I like to call a large amount of "X-factor," meaning that other people are genuinely interested in it and they want to hear your story. It makes you memorable.

I have been a college professor since 2004, and it is a thrill for me to now be "The Professor" who tells stories to students that excite them into action in their own lives. Without my original, inspirational professor, and that lucky chance to go to Belize, I have no idea where I would be today, and chances are that it wouldn't be nearly as satisfying. Archaeology is awesome!

CHAPTER 2

The History of Archaeology I: Scientists and Adventurers

Indiana Jones and the Possibilities of Things to Come

Indiana Jones and the Last Crusade came out when I was a junior in high school, during the time when students are beginning to take college seriously and think of potential schools where they might apply. Even though I was in an overcrowded theater sitting way too close to the screen, the third installment in the Indiana Jones trilogy was providing me with one of the most enjoyable cinematic experiences of my life. Although the movie delivered excitement, adventure and levity as Indiana Jones raced around the world searching for the Holy Grail, it was the final scene at the amazing archeological site of Petra that put it over the top for me. With the carved stone façade of Petra in the background, Indy and his friends jumped on their horses and raced away into the setting sun, leaving the Holy Grail for another day. As the theme song blared and the credits rolled, a possible career choice was added to the list in my brain. In the same moment, as I watched the other movie goers leave the theater, I realized that I was ready to leave home and go to college.

Indiana Jones: Scientist and Adventurer

Indiana Jones is the most famous archaeologist of them all. The iconic action hero portrayed by Harrison Ford set the cliché for how an archaeologist is supposed to look and behave. Leather jacket, satchel, whip, and trademark fedora hat is what Indy wears when he is ready for action! Real archaeologists don't wear that (those clothes would be way too hot!). Indiana Jones does all kinds of things that real archaeologists don't do, including destroying archaeology sites, ripping artifacts out of the ground without taking any measurements, and murdering bad guys. Even for all his archaeological transgressions, Indiana Jones is a major asset for our field. Indiana Jones is a fun, charismatic, dynamic, inspirational action hero that gets the general public interested in archaeology. Many of you reading this book probably picked it up because you thought that Indiana Jones was cool. There is nothing wrong with that! Now that you are here, it is up to me to show you how archaeology really works, but I thank Indy for getting you in the door. If an archaeologist tells you that they are completely uninspired by Indiana Jones, they are either (a) lying or (b) no fun at parties.

If we look a bit closer at Indiana Jones, we see that he symbolizes two cliches of "the archaeologist":

1. The nerdy **scientist**
2. The swashbuckling **adventurer**

Indy lives a dual life as the nerdy college professor at home and the swashbuckling, macho archaeologist while on an adventure. Much like Clark Kent changing into Superman, we see Indy as nerdy professor wearing a suit, glasses, and bow tie, while as adventurer, he changes into an open shirt, leather jacket, fedora, and is amazingly glasses-free! Although Indiana Jones is a fictional creation, the two overarching aspects to his character—the scientist and the adventurer—are what we can use as a jumping off point to discuss the beginnings of archaeology. Before archaeology was practiced as an academic discipline, there were those who made scientific breakthroughs (scientists) and those who explored the world to find new places (adventurers). Unfortunately, these adventurers rarely recorded their finds in an organized way, and often stole their finds in a "finders-keepers" style. Once the "adventurers" began to record their finds in a scientific, organized manner, we were able to use their artifacts as facts to tell meaningful stories about the past and archaeology was born. Who were these scientists and adventurers? Who gave us the building blocks on which archaeology is built on? Below, we will explore science first. Then we will look at early adventurers, and finally talk about how the two came together to form modern archaeology.

What is Science?—A Primer for Archaeology

In order to appreciate scientists, we want to ask ourselves "what is **science**?" When we think of "science," we think of Bunsen burners, lab coats, computers, and very difficult math. Science does not have to be complex—we can simply define it as "a way to reliably predict natural phenomena." At its base, that is all science is—an attempt to measure the processes that happen in the natural world. Many of us fear science because it seems complicated. Parts of it are fantastically complex, but the underlying idea is very simple.

Science is based on **empiricism**, which is the collection of facts about the world (data) that can be sensed or perceived by any of the five human senses (sight, touch, smell, hear, taste). This approach is not new—the Greeks did it 2,000 years ago, and it was refound and augmented during the Scientific Revolution of the 1500s. Since then, we have been practicing this way of figuring things out, which begins with **data**. Notice I did not say that science begins with **feelings**. Science does not care about your feelings. Your feelings are not important! You may really feel that you are right, but that does not matter. You must have data (facts about the material world) to prove that you are correct. Facts don't need you to believe in them.

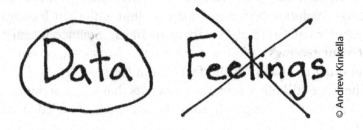

© Andrew Kinkella

There are two basic ways to practice science, called the **deductive method** and the **inductive method**. The deductive method is the classic hypothesis/testing style, where you come up with a possible reason to explain what you are seeing (a hypothesis), and then you test it (testing). The inductive method is based on looking for patterns. Here, you observe the natural world for a long time, looking for consistent patterns. Once those patterns are found, you then form a hypothesis to explain them. Neither method is better or "more sciency" than the other, these are simply two different ways of arriving at the same end. In my experience, I have seen the inductive method used more often in archaeology, as the search for patterns seems to follow naturally with archaeological mapping and excavation.

As we progress in the world of science, we see words like **law** and **theory** come up. A law in science is simply a universal constant (like the Law of Gravity). There is no controversy with laws in science. When was the last time you saw a gravity-denier? Unlike laws, certain scientific theories are beacons for public controversy. I find that the main reason for this is that the word "theory" has a public relations problem, largely based on the difference in meaning between how the general public uses the word "theory" and how scientists use it. Here is the difference:

1. In everyday speech, the word "theory" means a **guess**, such as when I say "My theory is that the window was broken sometime around 3 a.m."
2. In science, the word "theory" means an **explanation**. "The Theory of Evolution" is an explanation for evolution backed up by centuries of scientific testing, not a guess.

People who deny science conflate the two definitions, so you will hear them say things like "Evolution is *only* a theory." Some people don't like evolution because it doesn't align with their feelings, but remember what I said above about feelings? Science doesn't care about your feelings! We must have data. Archaeology must have data in order to discover solid facts about the past.

There are still other scientific concepts that we as archaeologists should appreciate. A **paradigm** is the accepted knowledge. This is different than a scientific law. This is simply a common truism that everyone agrees on. Ideas like the Earth is round or continents shift due to plate tectonics are paradigms. When we, as a society, change our collective mind (often due to new discoveries based on facts) that is called a **paradigm shift**. My favorite example of this is from several years ago, when Pluto was voted out as a planet. Pluto used to be a planet, but now it's not! This is because astronomers were finding many new "planetoids" like Pluto, which like Pluto were too small to really be considered planets. This brings up an interesting scientific question: Do you want Pluto back in the planet club? Don't you wish that little Pluto, out there far away by itself and all cold, could be welcomed back? I do too! But remember: Science does not care about your feelings! We assign feelings to Pluto because it is small, cold, and "cute" like a child in the snow. We want to take care of Pluto and we feel protective of it. Science says that you can't do that. Pluto is out. We as archaeologists must maintain this empirical focus and remember to be coldly honest with our data.

The last concept in our short overview of science is **Occam's Razor** (also called Occam's Rule). This belongs much more in the realm of philosophy than true science, but it is a useful concept to apply to archaeological theories as we try to explain the past. Occam's Razor states that all else being equal, the simplest explanation tends to be true. We want to apply this idea to archaeology and try to take the fewest steps to explain the artifacts that we find.

The Early Scientists

Although the Greeks are rightfully credited with many early scientific breakthroughs (such as figuring out the circumference of the Earth in 200 AD—amazing!), the beginnings of science as we know it today starts in the 1500s with the Enlightenment. For our needs in archaeology, we can divide early science into three broad categories:

1. **Astronomy/Physics**—The earliest scientists who gave us a general scientific framework for our world, talking about things like the Sun, planets, and gravity. Specifically:

Copernicus (1543)—The first modern scientist. The heliocentric theory, which means the Sun is the center of the solar system, not the Earth. He knew the Church would be angry, so he unveiled his theory on his death bed!

Galileo Galilei (early 1600s)—The other planets go around the Sun along with the Earth. The Church is pissed and forces him to live out the rest of his life under house arrest.

Issac Newton (late 1600s–early 1700s)—Figures out gravity along with many other important ideas, like the planets circle the sun in ellipses.

2. **Geology**—These scientists give us the proof that the Earth is not thousands of years old, but billions of years old. They also highlight the importance of stratigraphy.

    James Hutton and **Charles Lyell (late 1700s–early 1800s)**—Charles Lyell writes the first Geology book (*Principles of Geology*) in 1830 and guesses at the age of the Earth, based on stratigraphy, at 175 million years. They give us key ideas that we use in archaeology.

    Uniformitarianism—The idea that the natural process that we see today worked the same in the past.

    Stratigraphy—The soil and rock of the Earth's crust is constructed in layers that have been deposited over deep time.

    Superposition—The idea that deeper layers are older than shallower layers.

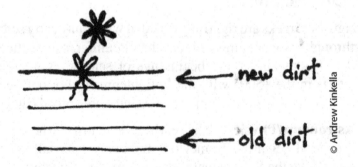

© Andrew Kinkella

3. **Biology**—These scientists give us evolution and the idea that creatures change over time to better fit their environment.
   Charles Darwin (mid 1800s)—Father of modern evolutionary theory. Writes *Origin of Species* in 1859 and gives us **evolution**—biological change over time based on the environment.

A science-based approach is the cornerstone of modern archaeology, which builds on the scientific foundation created by the scientists who came before us.

The Early Adventurers

On the opposite side from the early scientists, there is a group of people that I loosely call "The Adventurers." These are people who often possess extravagant personalities with great stories attached. I divide this group into three parts: **Looters, antiquarians, and explorers**.

Looters—These people are generally the worst. Out for personal gain, treasure hunting, breaking into tombs, stealing artifacts, and causing destruction and loss to the archaeological record.

Giovanni Belzoni (early 1800s)—The famous, flamboyant looter of Egypt. Although an unabashed looter, Belzoni had style! If you were having a party, you would probably invite him.

Antiquarians—Rich People who used their wealth to collect expensive artifacts and go on fabulous trips to famous archaeological sites. Usually focused on Old World places like Greece and Italy. They don't really exist anymore, but someone like William Randolph Hearst would be a close approximation.

Thomas Jefferson (late 1700s)—Not exactly an antiquarian, but an interesting person who excavated an ancient Native American mound on his property and was quite scientific for his day.

Explorers—in this category, I combine people who could be called "proto-archaeologists" with those who explored remote areas of the globe and happened to record archaeological sites while they were there.

Austin Henry Layard (mid-1800s)—worked in Mesopotamia in the 1840s, where he made his famous find of the Library at Nineveh.

John Lloyd Stephens and Frederick Catherwood (mid-1800s)—explored the Maya jungles of Central America. A lawyer and an artist who wrote about their journeys in several very popular travel books including *Incidents of Travel in Yucatan* (1843).

Heinrich Schliemann (1870s)—The famous discoverer of Homer's Troy and Mycenae (his finds actually pre-date the Trojan war by about 400 years). His lack of scientific excavation methods was a bit outdated even then.

The Scientists and Adventurers Together—The First Scientific Archaeologists

Now that we have explored the world of the scientist and the world of the explorer, it is time to put them together. Who was the first scientific archaeologist? My vote is **General Augustus Lane-Fox Pitt-Rivers**. Not only is his name fabulous to say, but he was also one of the first people to excavate an archaeological site using careful organization and recording techniques derived from science. He worked in the 1880s in England, focusing on Roman and Saxon sites. He was not there just to "find treasure," but would instead collect all the artifacts, even ordinary, everyday ones. Pitt-Rivers also took site preservation seriously, attempting to save sites throughout England from destruction. The work of Pitt-Rivers was generations ahead of people like Heinrich Schliemann, and really brings archaeology out of the darkness.

Other early archaeologists who worked in a scientific vein include **Sir Flinders Petrie**, known for his work in the 1880s Egypt, where he helped make strides in dating through examining Egyptian pottery and organizing it through careful seriation (see Chapter 9). Finally, **Howard Carter** would bring scientific archaeology to the attention of the world with his discovery of King Tut in 1922. His careful, methodological excavation of the Boy King which lasted for ten years brings us into the modern era. After this most famous archaeological find of all-time, the idea of using the scientific method in archaeology became the norm. In the Chapter 3, we will continue to trace the history of archaeology up to today, adding modern technology and the very important ingredient of anthropology into the archaeology mix.

Archaeological Example: King Tut

King Tutankhamun (nicknamed "King Tut") was a New Kingdom Pharaoh whose tomb was found in the Valley of the Kings by Howard Carter on November 23, 1922. King Tut ruled from 1332 to 1323 BC, during the eighteenth Dynasty of the New Kingdom. He is often referred to as "The Boy King" because he died when he was only 18, having suffered from ill health for years. As a pharaoh, he was not memorable, but as an archaeological find, he is immortal.

The tomb of King Tut is the most famous archaeological find of all time, and his spectacular gold death mask is probably the most famous artifact of all time. We are so fortunate that Howard Carter found it after years of painstaking archaeological research and spent an additional decade recording the contents of the tomb. Imagine if this had been found by looters, like every other tomb in the Valley of Kings? It is likely that we wouldn't know King Tut at all.

CHAPTER 3

The History of Archaeology II: Modern Archaeology and Anthropology

Maybe I'm Sick of Archaeology

I was on a plane. I don't remember where I was flying but I was definitely sick of archaeology. I had just finished my master's degree and applied to several part-time college teaching positions, all of which rejected me. The main reason I got a master's degree was to have the option to teach, and the rejection was extremely demoralizing. Maybe archaeology was not the career for me. I had worked in the Maya jungles and finished my degree. I looked out the window and thought "at least I have some good stories." A moment passed, and then I had another thought, "This is not all bad. At least I won't have to read any archaeological theory anymore! That stuff sucks!"

Modern History of Archaeology

The discovery and careful excavation of King Tut by Howard Carter marks the beginning of a more modern approach to archaeology, which centers around the **reconstruction of culture**. No longer focused on finding treasure or the shiniest artifacts, we are now using the ideas of anthropology to tell the story of the past more fully. As we learned in Chapter 1, since anthropology is the study of people, this is a good idea. Archaeologists will now conduct their research based upon a central **research question**, which helps to focus their studies. They will use archaeological **theory** to make their research question deeper and more meaningful to the human condition.

Finally, they will pick specific field **methods** that will help find the artifacts and data needed to answer the research question. Many of these ideas were used in earlier studies, but they were not done so in the organized fashion that we now experience.

What Is Culture?

The core idea that drives modern archaeology is the reconstruction of culture. What is culture? Before I give you the answer, **THINK**. What do you think of when I say the word "culture?" Although it's hard to define off the top of your head, I bet you think of things like different languages, clothes, food, places in the world, beliefs, and religions. These are all correct! We simply need to organize these examples of culture into a definition. According to my cultural anthropology textbook, culture is "Traditions and customs that govern behavior and beliefs; distinctly human; transmitted through learning" (Kottak 2016). Although this definition may sound complex, it's actually made up of three easy parts:

1. "Traditions and customs that govern behavior and beliefs"—This is all the stuff that you listed when I asked you to think about the word "culture." This is the easy part of culture that everyone understands, the beliefs/religions/clothes/food/language stuff.

2. "Distinctly human"—Although we may argue that chimpanzees, dolphins, and even ants have culture, no other animal comes close to the complexity of culture that human beings practice.

3. "Transmitted through learning"—Culture is learned! You are not born with culture. Even if you are born in Italy, you are not an Italian . . . yet. You must learn your beliefs, language, and traditions from your parents and your community. Culture is not biological.

When we look at these three parts of what makes culture, we see how important it is to the human experience. We might say that culture is the single defining characteristic of what makes us truly human. It becomes obvious why we would focus on this in archaeology in order to reconstruct the human experience of the past, but how do we see this in the dirt? The ancient people we study are all dead and gone, and all they have left us is their artifacts (also called "material culture" because humans made them). How do we take these lifeless objects and reconstruct life?

Reconstructing a Birthday Party

We will never know everything about what happened in the past and many things will be gone forever. Archaeology is our best hope for reconstructing a few precious pieces of culture by finding artifacts and analyzing them using the ideas of anthropology. As an example, let's reconstruct a child's birthday party. This sounds simple. Everyone knows what a birthday party is basically like, right? At the climax of the party, birthday candles are placed on a cake and lit, the lights are dimmed, the birthday party song is sung, the birthday person makes a wish, and the candles are blown out. Now imagine you are an archaeologist from 2,000 years in the future. Everyone who once knew what a birthday party was is long dead. The "birthday party" is a foreign, forgotten practice that took place in a language that nobody speaks anymore as part of a culture that has long ago vanished from the Earth. How do we reconstruct a "birthday party?"

We use anthropology. According to anthropology, a birthday party is a **ritual**. A ritual is "symbolic behavior that is socially standardized and repetitive. Both religious and secular, highly structured, and full of meaning." Like we did with culture, let's take a moment and break this down:

1. "Symbolic behavior that is socially standardized and repetitive"—Everyone in the society knows what these behaviors are ("standardized") and they are done at specific moments over and over ("repetitive").
2. "Religious and secular"—It can have religious meaning, but it doesn't have to.
3. "Highly structured and full of meaning"—There are many steps to the ritual, and it is a meaningful experience.

As defined by anthropology, a birthday party is a ritual practiced by our culture once a year (on the birthdate), where nonreligious, standardized steps are taken (cake, presents, song) in a meaningful way to celebrate and mark this important date. The birthday party ritual not only celebrates the person with the birthday, but it also strengthens family and community bonds as a reciprocal event (hopefully you will be invited to other people's parties).

To reconstruct this complex event, we need to find artifacts. Let's say that you have come across the remains of a house 2,000 years in the future. The house fell down during a disastrous earthquake which happened to occur during a birthday party. The people were able to get out, but all the birthday party artifacts were entombed in the house until you came across it 2,000 years later.

What is left from the birthday party ritual? Most things are gone or have rotted away—there are no people and no cake. What about the human cultural components like the song and the wish? Those were gone the moment the people stopped singing and wishing. As you excavate the remains of the house, you find a large serving plate, and some partially melted candles. You also find the remains of a plastic forks, knifes, and spoons. From the artifacts, you conclude that this was the site of a feasting ritual (the large serving plate and utensils), where human beings came together at a specific event to share food. The candles may have been used for light or maybe to keep the food warm!

Think about how much is missing. Things like the song and the wish will never be recovered. The idea that this event was for somebody's birthday is gone as well. Realize that modern archaeology is the same—how much are we missing, never to find? Everybody loves the reconstruction of ritual, as it is exciting stuff! If I reconstruct ancient diet (see Chapter 10) that data gives us important information but saying "they ate corn" is not nearly as exciting as saying "they sacrificed people to the corn god." Rituals are an exciting and dynamic part of the human experience, and whenever you can reconstruct even a small portion of one it is a deeply satisfying experience.

Does Theory Suck?

We covered the idea of a scientific theory in Chapter 2, discussing how the word "theory" means an "explanation." In academia, we gravitate towards explanations (theories) that we think make the most sense. When we look at our dataset, we can use different theories to highlight different aspects of the research. Some theories focus on the environment, whereas others will focus on human choices or the overall social structure of a society. Because archaeology is based on such little evidence, we can connect the dots in a practically unlimited number of ways. Although almost any theory will work to connect these dots, some work better than others. Most arguments in the academic world of archaeology are about which theory is the best. Unfortunately, this can take precedence over real archaeological work, where academics spend more time arguing about their favorite theory rather than spending time in the lab analyzing their artifacts!

What is Archaeological Theory?

Theories in archaeology have jargon-ridden names which makes them sound much more difficult than they actually are. Most of these can be separated into two groups—There are theories that can be seen as more "scientific" versus those that are more "humanities" in nature. Some "scientific" ones:

Environmental determinism
Human ecology
Systems theory
Processual archaeology

Some "humanities" ones:

Marxist archaeology
Feminist archaeology
Queer archaeology
Post-processual archaeology

These theories are used to set the framework for the archaeological project. They will inform how we plan and execute fieldwork in terms of where we will dig and what types of artifacts and data we will focus on. Underneath any theory that an archaeologist may be using, remember TLC! We are always wanting to know the timeline, the lifeways of the people, and important changes over time.

Is Archaeology a Science?

The best academic discussions are the ones that make people mad. As we have gone through the definition of archaeology as a science versus archaeology as a humanity, you must have come to some of your own conclusions. If you had to pick one, which camp do you belong with? Who are your people? Why?

THINK

Spend a moment and put yourself in the shoes of both. How does your camp change your perception of what archaeology is? How would your research questions change?

Since King Tut: Archaeology in Modern Times

Since the 1920s, archaeology has gone through a series of changes. Approximately every decade or so, a new technique or idea takes over the field and pushes everything into a new direction.

1940s—Dating Revolution

Dating techniques get much better, largely due to scientific advances made during World War II. We will explore this in Chapter 5.

1950s—Universities and Museums

Large, university and museum-driven archaeology projects are undertaken at famous, large sites. The focus is to understand the past and do good archaeology, but also to get impressive artifacts for the museums.

1960s–1970s—Science Rules!

A focus on the science side of archaeology with the idea that if we do science well enough, we can have a full understanding of the past. This is often referred to as "**objective**" or "**New Archaeology**" (although it came about during the 1960s). Because of the scientific focus, techniques such as **experimental archaeology** came into fashion. Experimental archaeology is where exact replicas of ancient tools (such as a bow and arrow or an axe) are made and used today to see how well they work. The downside of this style of archaeology is that it can actually get too "sciency," meaning that the story of the past can get lost in scientific minutia. Sometimes, there are too many measurements and spreadsheets and not enough humanity.

1980s–1990s—Humanities Rule!

A reaction against the overly scientific archaeology of the 1970s, the 1980s bring us a focus on the humanities. This is called the "**postmodern**" or "**subjective**" or "**post-processual**" approach. It is more focused on individual stories and multiple possibilities for the stories of the past. There is a reactionary attitude of deconstruction of what came before, as researchers used less cold science and more warm feelings and ideas. The questions asked about the past here are very interesting, high-level and dynamic. The downside to this style of archaeology is that the questions can get too far away from the actual data, and it becomes all feelings and few facts.

Today—Nobody Rules!

The best archaeology practiced today uses the solid scientific approach of the 1970s "New Archaeology" and combines it with the more interesting human questions of the 1980s "postmodern" era. This is sometimes referred to as "cognitive archaeology." We follow the six steps of archaeology (see Chapter 6) and use our finds to tell the story of the past. It is a great time to be an archaeologist!

© Andrew Kinkella

Archaeological Example

Stonehenge is a great archaeological example to use when discussing theory. A solstice marker in England made of huge carved stones that is approximately the same age as the pyramids (about 4,500 years old). We can analyze Stonehenge from a scientific side, focusing on where the stones are from and how it was constructed. We can also look at Stonehenge from a more humanities side, asking what it meant to the ancient people who lived there. We can see the give-and-take at work when we compare a scientific description of Stonehenge to a humanities description of Stonehenge—the scientific side has more data and facts, but may be less satisfying, whereas the humanities approach is much more satisfying but relies on thinner facts and more guesswork and interpretation.

CHAPTER 4

Why Archaeology Sites are Still Here: Context and Preservation

A Pile of Stones and the Right-Handed Stone Tool Maker

I had experienced brutally hot days on archaeology projects in the desert, and luckily this wasn't one of them. Although the air was bone dry, the temperature was pleasant as we walked along in the surprisingly comfortable desert sun. I was part of a small archaeology crew whose job it was to survey miles of land along the California/Arizona border looking for archaeological sites that would be destroyed by a pipeline that was going to be built in the area. I hadn't seen anything that day until the unmistakable glint of glassy stone caught my eye, sitting at the foot of a small boulder. The boulder was about four feet high and of excellent shape for sitting, so I walked over and sat on it! A good place to sit today was a good place to sit thousands of years ago. I instantly understood why the small pile of broken, glassy stone was on the ground next to my right foot—it was left over from making a stone tool. Somebody had sat exactly where I was sitting sometime centuries ago and spent the afternoon shaping a stone tool. As they shaped the tool, they let the flakes that were popping off fall to the ground, as they had no need for small scraps of stone. When they were done, they took the finished tool with them, leaving the small pile of left-over scraps. This was an archaeological site at its most elemental—a specific spot where a person had spent an afternoon engaged in an activity, and left artifactual evidence of what happened. Luckily for me, the artifacts were stone and were tough enough to preserve for centuries in the desert.

I realized that I was sitting in the exact place that the person had sat, but simply at a different time. I felt like a time traveler who had accidentally materialized into someone else's body, sharing body and soul for a split second. As I took in the moment, I realized something else. The ancient person was right-handed. If they were left-handed, the pile of stones would have been on the other side of the boulder! I had never used the location of artifacts to figure out something that specific before. I hopped off the boulder, recorded the site of the right-handed stone tool maker, and walked onward into the mild desert day.

Top Ten Key Terms!

In the two previous chapters, we learned about the history of archaeology. Now we turn our attention to how archaeology is practiced today. How do we "do" archaeology in the twenty-first century? Before we pick up our trowel, we need to know the language. Archaeology has some basic key terms that you will hear used multiple times on any archaeological project (and I have probably already used half of them in earlier chapters!). In order to make things easy, I have provided a list below that we can call *the Top Ten Key Terms in Archaeology*.

1. **Artifact**—Material remains left over from previous cultures (a "piece of the past"). An artifact is any human-made or modified object. In practice, it's usually small enough that it can be carried. The term **material culture** is also used to describe artifacts, and the terms are often used interchangeably. I prefer the term "artifact," as I find "material culture" overly complicated.

2. **Potsherd**—A broken piece of pottery. You will also hear the term "potshard," but "potsherd" is more correct.

3. **Assemblage**—This is the sum total of all artifacts found at a site. Everything from the prettiest intact vase to the smallest broken potsherd. If we were talking about King Tut, the assemblage would be everything found in his tomb. A **Subassemblage** is a defined portion of the total assemblage. If I was studying King Tut's tomb, I could look at the subassemblage of gold artifacts, or the subassemblage of hunting equipment.

4. **Feature**—This concept is classically difficult for my students. The best way to think of a feature is as a thing that loses its integrity when moved. A gargoyle on the exterior of a building is a feature. In our modern culture, an outside basketball court is a feature. Most importantly for archaeology, a **burial** is a feature and so is a **hearth** (the remains of a fire pit). A feature is often a specific piece of something larger, but not always.

5. **Midden**—I like to think of a midden as a mix or "heap" of artifacts. It can also be seen as an artifact scatter. In some areas, a midden simply means a trash pit. Middens can be small like a simple trash pit, or very large. The remains of an entire village, mixed and broken due to centuries of weathering, eroding, and human-caused destruction, can be seen as a midden.

6. **Structure**—A building. A pyramid, temple, or house are all structures.

7. **Mound**—Usually the ruins of an ancient structure (such as a house mound), or sometimes a simple pile of earth (such as a burial mound).

8. **Site**—A bounded area where cultural events took place. Sites can be any size. In the "desert stone tool maker" example at the beginning of this chapter, that site is only a few square feet in size, whereas the Pyramids of Giza in Egypt are part of a huge site many acres across.

9. **Isolate**—A lone artifact, found by itself, not a part of any site.

10. **Culture Area**—The largest defined area for archaeology, usually defined by the language spoken by the people at the time. The Maya, Egypt, and Inca are all culture areas.

The Vital Importance of Context

Now that we have some important basic key terms in our toolbox, we can begin to discuss larger concepts. A great concept to start with is **context**. Context is the location of an artifact in time and space including what it is found *in* and what it is found *with*. We can divide context into three parts:

1. **Matrix**—The material that the artifact is found in. This may be dirt (soil), water, ice, sand, and even air (for example, if the artifact is found in a dry cave on the surface).
2. **Association**—What the artifact is found with. This can include other artifacts and also the specific layer of dirt (strata) that the artifact is in.
3. **Provenience**—The specific location in time and space of the artifact on the Earth. We can record this using a GPS, latitude and longitude coordinates, depth measurements under the surface, and so on.

When we put together matrix, association, and provenience (MAP), we have the context of the artifact. Context is massively important. One of the worst parts of looting is that it destroys the context of the artifacts. When we don't know where the artifact is from, what it was found in, and what it was found with, we don't have much information at all. Very little can be added to the story of the past. I see local news stories every so often about a person who donates their collection of looted artifacts to a local museum. The story often gives a very positive spin to the person who donates their collection (as a virtuous giver), but these people have bought (or stolen) looted artifacts over the years, destroying our past and obliterating any context that those artifacts once had. These artifacts are not worth much to those of us who are trying to tell the story of the past, as so much of their story is missing. We would have known so much more if these artifacts were not illegally ripped from their location and sold. The people who collect these artifacts and then grow a conscious years later are not virtuous. They are thieves of our shared human past.

Context is so important that we define it in two different ways, as **primary context** or **secondary context**. Primary context is defined as "point of last discard." That means that we find the artifact exactly where it was left thousands of years before (also referred to as "in situ"). Secondary context is when an artifact is found in a different location from where it was originally left. It may have been moved by erosion, flooding, weather, animals, or humans. Both context types are affected by **taphonomy**, which is the natural and cultural events that affect the artifact after it has been left behind. The only difference between the two context types in regards to taphonomy is that secondary context artifacts were ultimately moved, and primary context artifacts were not moved.

Context and Grandma

Let's try a thought experiment to illustrate context: Later today, you get a call. It's your mom, and she has some bad news. Apparently, your grandmother has died. She was at home on the couch, watching her favorite show when she had a massive heart attack and died. Her death was immediate. Then the ambulance came, and your grandma was transported to the morgue, and ultimately to the funeral home. Two days later, you had her memorial service, which was open casket. After that, she was taken to the cemetery where your family had a final service and then she was buried next to grandpa.

Is grandma in primary or secondary context?

THINK.

DON'T SKIP AHEAD!

THINK.

Grandma is in primary context! Remember that primary context is *point of last discard*. Although grandma died at home, we were not done with her yet as a society and as a culture. We still had several important death rituals that we needed to do with her body before we were ready to let her go. If we find out later that grandma may have been killed by the next door neighbor, we will then exhume her body and study it for possible clues. When we then re-bury her (even if it's in the same spot), she will then be in secondary context.

The Importance of Preservation

We also want to look at **preservation**. What preserves an archaeology site best? When I ask this question, we immediately think of famously preserved archaeological sites, like King Tut or the Ice Man. King Tut is in a hot, dry area whereas the Ice Man is in a cold, icy area, yet both are preserved excellently. These examples seem like opposites. How does this make sense? The key here is that in both cases the temperatures stayed constant for thousands of years. The hot or the cold doesn't matter that much. What matters is that the conditions stay the same and don't vary.

Think of your refrigerator. Your refrigerator is a preservation device—it keeps things cold and stable. What happens when the electricity goes out? Your fridge becomes disgusting very quick! The food rots at what seems to be an incredible rate. Have you ever opened a fridge up after it being unplugged for a week? You find levels of disgusting that you never thought possible. This is because not only is the food no longer cold, but it has also lost its stable environment.

Good conditions for preservation are **constant**. Bad conditions are **variable**.

Preservation Device

© Andrew Kinkella

EXAMPLES: Pompeii and the Ice Man.

Pompeii—Italian village covered by volcanic ash from the eruption of Vesuvius in 79 AD. Because of the excellent preservation provided by this cataclysmic event, we are able to see what people ate, and even what artwork they painted on the walls of their houses.

The Ice Man—Found by hikers in the Alps on the border between Austria and Italy in 1991. Found to be 5,300 years old (about a thousand years older than the Egyptian pyramids!). Because of his excellent preservation, his tools, clothes, and even the contents of his stomach give us all kinds of great information about life in Bronze Age Italy. We can even see his 61 tattoos!

CHAPTER 5

Dating the Past

Carbon-14 Dating Is Awesome, But Human Beings (Including Me) Are Fallible

I have taught generations of students that they should always believe their own Carbon-14 dates. In class, I rant about how ignorant people deny the facts of Carbon-14, mainly because they just don't like the date that came back. Usually, the denial comes from religious reasons, but sometimes scientists themselves will deny their own dates because they don't want to believe that their hypothesis is wrong.

I pride myself on being data-driven and not letting my feelings get in the way of any archaeological work that I may be doing, but something strange happened a few years ago. When I got my Carbon-14 dates back from a site that I had worked at for years, they didn't seem to make any sense. They were way too recent. I was expecting the dates to land somewhere in the vicinity of a thousand years old, but these dates were much younger, only 300 years old or so. I immediately thought the samples must have been contaminated. How could I have been so stupid as to mess up my own samples? I thought I had been careful, but apparently not! There is no way that part of the site could be that recent.

I sent in a second batch. This time I was extremely careful. I touched nothing with bare hands, and each precious shell fragment that I was using to date was lovingly placed in tinfoil using tweezers, which was then placed in two plastic bags. With the care of a new parent, I packed the box with extra packing material and sent it on its way. Several weeks later the dates came back. They were all the same!!!!! Three hundred years old, give-or-take. There was no problem with the samples. The problem was with me. I didn't believe my own dates. I was one of those ignorant scientists who didn't want to believe that their hypothesis was wrong! See how insidious our own belief systems are? I had nothing to lose no matter how the dates came back. I was simply trapped in my preconceived notion of how old that section of the site was "supposed" to be.

The moral of the story is to believe your own dates. Science works. Don't let your personal beliefs, wants, and feelings interfere with your research. If it's not what you expect, roll with it! The new answers to new questions will be the most exciting answers of all.

The Measurement of Time

Measuring time is an odd thing. Think about it. What is time anyway? When are we right now? I wrote these words months or years ago at this point where you are currently reading them. Where am I right now, the author who wrote these words? Did time catch up with me? Am I dead? When are you right now in comparison to me? The measurement of time is very meaningful in archaeology. What is the first question that people ask about an archaeological site? Likely "How old is it?" In this chapter, we will explore how to tell time, and then how to date archaeological sites based on what we find there.

We reckon time in our mind in two basic ways: as **linear** and **cyclical**. Linear time has a beginning point and runs straight into the future. In our calendar, the years are linear. They count up from an agreed upon start date, such as the birth of Jesus. We also experience cyclical time, which is cycles that repeat themselves over and over, such as days of the week and seasons. Both linear and cyclical time are examples of **chronology**, which is simply how we as humans make sense of the passage of time. Although both chronologies are useful in explaining our lives, archaeological dating methods are concerned with linear time, as we are trying to figure out how long ago something happened.

Dating Methods

There are two basic categories of archaeological dating: **Relative dating methods** and **absolute dating methods**. Relative dating methods rely on comparisons between artifacts, where you can say that one is older or younger than the other, but you may not know the actual age of anything. Common relative dating methods include:

Stratigraphy—The ultimate old-school dating method! Simply using the layers of earth as a guide, and making a guess based on how deep the artifact is and what type of layer it was found in.

Seriation—If we have a master list of artifact style changes through time and we use that to date a site, that is called **seriation**.

The Three Age System—Stone Age, Bronze Age, and Iron Age are the three "ages" used in this method, based on the types of tools found at the site. Useful only in the Old World and very general.

Absolute Dating Methods

Carbon-14 dating, also known as C-14 or radiocarbon dating, is the dating workhorse of archaeology. All of the other dating methods are secondary to this one. This is because Carbon-14 dating is relatively cheap (at around 350 bucks per sample), relatively easy (you only need a few grams of organic material), and relatively accurate (plus or minus 50 years or so). I love Carbon-14 dating!

Material needed: Organic material, such as charcoal, bone, or shell.

Accuracy: Plus or minus 30–200 years, depending on location and age.

Range: Modern back to 75,000 years or so.

Usually used for: Any location that needs a date and has organic material. Most archaeological sites.

In order to understand how Carbon-14 works, we need to first look at Carbon-12, which is "regular" carbon. If you look on a periodic chart, Carbon is number six, meaning it has six protons and six neutrons, which gives you an atomic weight of 12. But if you look at the bottom of the chart, you see that Carbon's atomic weight is listed as 12.01124. What's the deal with the ".012124?" Carbon's weight is not exactly 12 because every so often, there are **isotopes** of Carbon that exist in the world. An isotope of Carbon would be like Carbon-13 or -14. Carbon-13 has one extra neutron. Carbon-14 has two extra neutrons. These isotopes are like an exotic jungle disease, meaning that they are rare but always around. More importantly, all living things have a bit of Carbon-14 in them. This little bit of Carbon-14 gets replenished every day, as we eat, breathe, and generally interact with our world. Everything is fine until we die.

Once we die (and by "we," I mean any plant or animal), our Carbon-14 begins to decay. The beauty of this whole story is that the decay can be measured very precisely. Luckily for archaeologists everywhere, Carbon-14 decays by a process called **half-life**, where 5,730 years from the day you die, your body will contain exactly half as much Carbon-14 as it did when you were alive. In two half-lives (a.k.a. 11,460 years from the day you die), your body will contain exactly one quarter as much Carbon-14 as it did when you were alive. Three half-lives? One eighth is left. And so on.

Trick question—When do we run out of Carbon-14?

THINK . . .

Answer—Never, but after about 75,000 years, the amount left gets too small to measure.

Can Carbon-14 be wrong? Asking if Carbon-14 can be wrong is like asking if an AIDS test can be wrong. The answer is yes, but it is very, very rare (although a friend of mine did indeed get a false positive AIDS test once—whoa!). It's more common for Carbon-14 to be a little off, based on local environmental factors where the sample was collected. These environmental factors mean that a Carbon-14 date needs to be calibrated to take the local conditions into account. In reality, this means adding a few years in some places, or subtracting years in others. Carbon-14 date calibration can get fantastically complex, and that is where small errors most commonly occur, but these are very minor (for example, your date might be 50 years off, not 5,000 years off). For science, Carbon-14 is a rock-solid method of dating the past. The most common reason for a nonbelief in C-14 results is simply because the researcher doesn't want to believe the results, like my example at the beginning of this chapter.

There are two general types of Carbon-14 testing. The first one is called "Radiocarbon dating" (a.k.a. "the regular way") where a marble-sized piece of material is burned up in order to measure the remaining amount of Carbon-14 and get a date. The second method is called Accelerator Mass Spectrometry (a.k.a. "AMS," or "the expensive way") where a much smaller piece of material can be used. AMS is generally about twice the price of a standard Radiocarbon date, but worth it if you only have very small bits of material, or the material is so precious that destroying more than the smallest bit would be counterproductive. In the last few years, AMS is getting much cheaper (around 400 dollars per sample) and old-school radiocarbon dating is being phased out.

What sucks about Carbon-14?

1. It isn't completely exact (there is a plus or minus 100 years or so there).
2. It only works on organic material.
3. There can be problems with calibration, and a date may be off by a few years.
4. Although one of the cheaper dating methods, several hundred bucks per sample is still expensive!

Even with these drawbacks, in the end Carbon-14 is still great. It is far and away the best and most popular dating method out there for archaeology. All the other methods listed from now on place a far second to the overwhelming utility of Carbon-14.

Potassium–Argon (K–Ar) and Argon–Argon

Potassium–Argon and Argon–Argon dating are very similar. They work in the same general method as Carbon-14, where the half-life is measured as Potassium degrades into Argon in the case of Potassium–Argon, and where one form of Argon degrades into another form of Argon in the case of Argon–Argon. Here, the half-life is 1.25 billion years!

> Material needed: ancient lava flows. Only works if you are in an area with volcanoes.

> Accuracy: Plus or minus 100,000 years.

> Range: From several hundred thousand years ago to billions of years ago.

> Usually used for: The oldest events on Earth, such as dinosaurs, geologic time periods, beginnings of life on Earth.

Dendrochronology

Dendrochronology is tree ring dating. The word itself seems difficult, but it's actually quite easy ("Dendro" means trees, and "chrolology" means time measurement, so "Dendrochronology" means "tree-time measurement"). Since tree rings are made every year, they trace the environmental history of the area. Years with heavy rain make fat tree rings, and years of drought make skinny rings. Therefore, the specific pattern of rings from a given tree piece can be matched to the overall environmental history of the area, and the exact year the tree died can be surmised. In order to make this work, we need to find wood at the site (usually in the form of charcoal), and we need a master chart of tree rings by year that we can compare with our sample. What's great about tree ring dating is that we can get the exact year that the tree died by figuring out where the piece fits on the master chart. On the downside, the master chart of tree ring variability is rare or nonexistent for most areas in the world. If you are able to use tree rings, great! Unfortunately, you probably won't have them.

> Material needed: a piece of a tree with rings from an area where the tree ring history is known.

> Accuracy: To the exact year the tree died.

> Range: Recent time back to 10,000 years or so.

Usually used for: great dates for sites from places like the American Southwest.

Problems with Dating

The **Old Wood Problem** happens when the wood found at the site is older than the site itself. This happens because people tend to reuse really good pieces of wood. For example: I cut a tree down in 1000 AD and use it as the main beam of my house. 100 years later (in 1100 AD), the house falls down but the beam is still good. My ancestors use the same beam for their new house which they build that same year in 1100AD. That house falls down in a huge earthquake in 1200 AD, trapping everyone inside. An archaeologist finds the remains of my dead ancestors in the house and takes a sample of the beam to date the site. The date comes back as 1000 AD (the year the tree was cut) but the earthquake was in 1200 AD! That's because the wood was saved and recycled in new houses several times. The Old Wood Problem always dates a site falsely older than it really is.

The **Heirloom Effect** is a similar problem, but this happens when people keep heirlooms from their ancestors (objects that tend to stay in a family over generations like watches, fine china, etc.). Like the old wood problem, these objects will date the site older than it actually is. For example: My great grandfather buys a brand-new watch in 1917 at a small watch shop in France during World War I. He survives the war and passes it on to his son (my grandfather) in 1943 as a good luck charm when his son goes off to fight in World War II. My grandfather survives as well and passes it onto my father in 1972 when he goes to fight in Vietnam. My father survives and passes on the watch to me in 1991 as a family heirloom. I never go to war, but instead die in a freak bass fishing accident in 2021 with the watch on my wrist.

Archaeologists find my remains a thousand years later and use the watch on my wrist to date my remains to . . . 1917! They conclude I died in my freak bass fishing accident in 1917. WRONG! I died in 2021 but happened to be wearing a watch that was much older than I was—this is the heirloom effect in action. Luckily, in real-world archaeology, we usually find multiple artifacts at a site and can date many of them. We will notice the heirlooms as outliers. In that instance, they are fun to find because it shows that the people of the past thought that the object was important enough to keep for a long time.

Other Dating Methods

There are many other dating methods that may be used, including:

Thermoluminescence—measures when an object was last heated to very high temperatures.

Obsidian Hydration—measuring the amount of water vapor trapped inside the surface of a piece of obsidian. The more water, the longer it's been since the stone was chipped.

There are many more. I have not listed them here, because in my experience, these methods are not used often in archaeology. It doesn't mean that they are never used or are bad! It just means that they are not common.

A Moment on Written Records

Written records are fantastic except for one fact: Human beings are a bunch of liars! Written records are rare in archaeology, and it is a huge treat if a site happens to have some. They can include written language on paper or stone. Although it seems like written records are the ultimate in dating, sometimes it's not so obvious . . .

THOUGHT EXPERIMENT:
Written Records and Fallible Humans

Have you or a friend or family member ever backdated a check? I KNOW YOU HAVE. You are a liar! You have created a false written record. Have you cheated on your taxes? More false written records created by liars! Here is an example of how your lying ways affect the archaeological record: You rent and apartment and the rent is due on the first of the month. You are a responsible person and pay the rent every month on the first. But then in December, you happen to have a lot going on in your life. You wake up on the 5th of December, and the realization sends a shockwave through your body. "Oh crap! I forgot the rent!" You jump out of bed, grab your checkbook, and furiously fill it out.

Except for the date. What date do you write in?

THINK.

BE HONEST!

THINK.

Do you write December 1st into the date line? NO! You write November 30th, as if you were not only on time, but you were a day early! You my friend are a liar and a producer of incorrect written records, just like me, and just like all the people of the past! Remember that the people of the past are just like you. They have good days, bad days, and sometimes they just need to tell a bit of a white lie to make the day go by a little smoother.

Written records are great! Mostly.

Example of Dating: The History of Everything

Welcome to the last 13 billion years at a glance! Here are the top ten most important moments for human beings and their relationship to the Earth and the universe. All of these things needed to happen to place you where you are right now, reading this book as a modern human. We are so fortunate that not only do we know about these important moments, but thanks to modern dating methods we also know *when* they happened.

Top Ten Most Important Moments in Human History

1. **Big Bang**: You need a universe to live in. Happened at 12.9 billion years ago. Dated using the speed of light and the Doppler Effect, among other things.
2. **Formation of Earth**: You need a planet to live on. Formed 4.6 billion years ago. Dated using Potassium–Argon.
3. **Life on Earth**: You need to be a living organism. First life happened approximately 3.8 billion years ago. Dated using Potassium–Argon.
4. **Rise of Mammals**: You are a mammal. First mammals evolved around 100 million years ago. Dated using Potassium–Argon.
5. **First Human Ancestors**/Bipedalism in Africa: You are a human who walks on two legs. Our oldest ancestors are about 6–7 million years old. Dated using Potassium–Argon (Volcanic layer in East Africa).
6. **Out of Africa**/Human Diaspora: You are a world-wide phenomenon, and most of you live on continents besides Africa. We leave Africa around 1.5 million years ago, during the Pleistocene. Dated using Potassium–Argon.

7. **The Upper Paleolithic Revolution**: You are an advanced *Homo sapiens* who uses complex tools and engages in complex belief systems including making art and burying your dead in meaningful ways. Begins approximately 50,000 years ago. Dated using Carbon-14.
8. **Peopling of the New World**: You either live in the New World or know somebody who does. Begins at approximately 17,000 years ago. Dated using Carbon-14, and seriation.

9. **The Neolithic Revolution**: You live in a culture that is ultimately supported by farming and there are cities nearby. Begins around 10,000 years ago. Dated using Carbon-14, seriation, dendrochronology, and written records.
10. **The Industrial Revolution**: You live in a culture that is utterly dependent on fossil fuels (although we are trying to get away from them!). Begins around 1850 AD. Dated using written records.

PART TWO

Doing Archaeology in the Field

Congratulations! You have made it through the first third of your archaeological education. Welcome to the second third, where we learn how archaeology is done, from the first day on the dig to the last day of lab clean up. Specifically, we will go through the planning, mapping, excavation, lab work, and final write-up of a typical archaeological project.

CHAPTER 6

Organizing an Archaeological Expedition and Preparing for the Trip

Project Beginnings and Endings

It was finally my time. I had heard of a shipwreck of the coast of Belize that had never been recorded by an archaeology crew. If I wrote a research proposal and got the proper permits and money, I could lead my own archaeology crew in Belize for the first time. I had worked on many archaeology projects in Belize over the previous 20 years and had underwater archaeology experience. I had professional connections and I knew what was necessary to write a successful research proposal. I knew I could do this! I spent several months carefully constructing a focused research question, assembling a skilled crew with advanced scuba certifications, and acquiring a small amount of funding. I sent my proposal in to the Institute of Archaeology in Belize and awaited the green light to start leading an underwater archaeology project on a shipwreck on Belize's barrier reef.

I was denied.

Due to unforeseen environmental impacts that were affecting the barrier reef that summer, all underwater research of any kind was suspended. My project was over before it began. There was nothing else to do except try again the next year. It was embarrassing to tell the crew what happened, and it made me feel like a loser.

How to Run an Archaeology Project: The Six Steps

How do you plan, run, and finish an archaeological project? As we can see from my sad story above, and archaeology project is a fragile creature that can fall apart at any time. An archaeologist needs to be a careful shepherd of their project, making sure that it moves forward in a professional, timely manner. In this chapter, we are going to explore the nuts and bolts of getting an archaeological project up and running and follow the steps from the very beginning until the final wrap up, a process that usually takes years. As the next several chapters deal with the real process of "doing" archaeology, we will use my PhD dissertation experience (focusing on the ancient Maya) as a template and example to illustrate the process.

We will also explore the mental experience and day-to-day needs of preparing for an archaeological project. If the project you will work on is far from home, it is important to pack well for an extended trip into an environment that you may not be familiar with. It is also extremely important to be mentally prepared for a trip that may test your psyche to the extremes. You may feel the greatest joy, excitement, and personal pride on an archaeology project, but this elation may be tempered with feelings of loneliness, selfishness, and depression. I am not here to scare you, but merely to make you prepared for what is coming.

This process of archaeological research can be broken into six steps: research design, set up, field work, lab work, interpretation, and publication. A working knowledge of these steps is central to your understanding of archaeology and provides a framework for the key concepts of the next several chapters. Each step has several important aspects to it, so pay close attention here! The division of the steps into six is not a hard and fast rule. What matters is the general flow of events that must happen for an archaeological project to be a success:

a. **Research Design**—Deciding on a research question and writing it up.
b. **Set Up**—Getting permits, funding, and a crew.
c. **Field Work**—"Doing archaeology"—gathering data through survey, mapping, and excavation.
d. **Lab Work**—Processing, analyzing, organizing, and recording the artifacts.
e. **Interpretation**—Answering the research question and telling the story.
f. **Publication**—Publishing your results.

Following is a detailed description of each step:

1. **Research Design**

An archaeology project begins with a question about the past. This **research question** can be anything, like how long did Maya kings rule, or how important was corn to the diet, or when did the culture change from foraging to farming. It needs to be focused and specific enough that it can be answered by the artifacts that you may possibly find in the area where you will be working. A solid research question makes everything else flow more smoothly, as the common goal of the project will be that much more obvious. Realize that it is okay if your research question is not answered! Research questions are often changed, edited, or expanded upon as new artifacts are uncovered. Archaeology is a dynamic practice where we never know exactly what kind of data we will find until we find it! A relaxed ability to improvise as the season progresses is a valuable skill. For me, my research question was "How did the ancient Maya use cenotes in their daily lives, and how did the cenotes relate to the nearby cities and towns?" (Cenotes are small, deep freshwater lakes in the jungle). I came up with this question because there happened to be 25 cenotes in the study area where I worked in Belize, and I wanted to learn more about them and relate them to the Maya sites nearby.

After the research question is solidified, the archaeologist will have to do a large amount of **background research** to make sure that they are not asking a question that has already been answered. In my case, I spent long hours in the library and online researching my topic. I also listened to my professors who gave me great advice on books and articles to read. I ended up reading a lot about water ritual, archaeological site survey, scuba diving practices, the Classic Period of the ancient Maya (especially in Belize), and the relationship between cenotes and caves. I got a very good feel for the research that had been done up to that point, and I was sure that I would not be rehashing somebody else's idea.

When your research question is set and your background research is done, you will now write up a formal plan for how you will carry out your research, called a **research design**. Here you state your research question and why this question is important, how it will fit into current studies in your area, and how you will go about answering it. You will talk about where and when you will be conducting your research, how much money and equipment you need, and who you will be working with. *The research design is a blueprint for the entire project.* All choices made on the project must flow from the research design. Much like the research question, the better the research design is the smoother the project will go.

2. Set Up

Now it is time to put the project in motion. In the set-up phase, we will need three things to implement our research design: a **permit** to do archaeological research, **money** to pay for the project, and a **crew** to do the work.

A permit is serious business. An archaeologist can never "just start digging" wherever they would like, even if they have a PhD. They have to apply for a permit though the correct agency which is usually a government agency or the landowner. Even if all of your paperwork is professional and your research proposal is excellent, the permit can still be denied for a variety of reasons outside of your control.

Getting money for an archaeological project is often done by applying for grants from government agencies. The most familiar of these to archaeologists is the National Science Foundation (commonly referred to as the NSF). We apply for the money by filling out paperwork and sending in our research design. Competition for this money is fierce and chances of getting an NSF are low. If your project gets funded by the NSF, that is very impressive! There are many other funding agencies, including well-known ones like the National Geographic Society (NGS). You may even get lucky and get money from a rich person. Important note—never use your own money. Archaeology projects can become very expensive.

The third and final piece of the "Set Up" phase is to assemble an archaeological crew. The crew can vary in size from a handful of individuals to dozens of people, but the organization of a crew usually follows this structure:

1. The **Primary Investigator (P.I.)**—This is the lead archaeologist. They usually have a PhD, and they are responsible for the research design and getting the money and the permit. They will direct the project, and their name will be first on the major publications to come from the research.

2. The **Field Director**—The second in command. This person is in the field every day, directing the daily work of the crew and solving problems. Usually, the Field Director and the P.I. work closely together, discussing the direction of the project and bouncing ideas off each other.

3. The **Lab Director**—This person stays in the on-site lab and makes sure all the artifacts are organized and being processed in a timely manner.

4. **Specialists**—An archaeology project does not have only archaeologists on it! Specialists such as botanists, architects, photographers, biologists, osteologists, ceramicists, and geologists will stop by for a short time to do specialized studies that relate to the archaeology site. It's great for the crew to get a different perspective on the past that these people bring with them.

5. **The Crew**—Usually made up of a mix of students and local people hired by the P.I., the crew is the essential workforce that makes archaeology possible. This also includes a cook (a good cook on an archaeology project is a godsend). Archaeologists usually begin their careers as

© Andrew Kinkella

crewmembers as part of a "field school." This entry-level spot is where we all learn the skillset needed to become archaeologists.

3. Field Work

This is the fun part! We have finished our research design, our permits are in order, and our crew is ready. It's time to do archaeology! This part begins as we pack our bags for the trip out to the site. This may be a simple day trip or a months-long excursion to a different country. For the longer trips, I have made a checklist that I hand out to my students before they leave. I have included it at the end of this chapter to give you an idea of how an archaeologist packs for an expedition.

Once at the site, we will be spending our days surveying for new sites, mapping in the sites we have already found, and excavating at the sites that will best answer the questions posed in our research design. This is often hard work in inclement conditions, but it is exciting and extremely satisfying. We will also be filling out excavation paperwork, drawing maps, and collecting artifacts in an organized manner to prepare them for later analysis in the lab.

4. Lab Work

Now back from the field, it is time to organize, process, analyze, and record the artifacts found by the project. Unfortunately, this is where many archaeology projects go to die (more on this in Chapter 9). This is often the single longest step of all six, with many hours spent in the lab weighting, measuring, and processing the artifacts for entry into a catalog. Once the artifacts are recorded, they are prepared for long-term storage.

5. Interpretation

After we have excavated the site and analyzed our artifacts, it is time to answer our research question based on the data we found. The answer will then help us tell a new and improved story of the past. This new data will augment the story and give us insights into the past that we never had before. One of the most exciting moments in archaeology is when the data that you have painstakingly found begins to unravel the story of the past before your eyes! We will be writing this story down with an eye towards publishing it, so other people can benefit from our work.

6. Publication

Once the story of the past is written down, the final step is to publish it. It is not necessary for the published work to be an

Amazon best seller; it simply needs to be accessible to the next generation of archaeologists so they can find it during their research design phase and build upon the good work that you have done. Several common ways of publishing the final report:

1. **Grey Literature**—The easiest but least satisfying method. A handful of final reports are printed, bound, and given to local archaeological information centers, local historical interest groups, the landowner, and possibly local universities (the archaeologist will of course keep a few copies for themselves). Because so few copies are in existence, these can be very hard to locate in the future.

2. **Academic Journals**—The most academically prestigious method. Academic journals are usually published four times a year. They are collections of academic articles that are very professionally done yet almost impossible for the general public to understand. Examples include *American Antiquity* which is published by the Society for American Archaeology (SAA) and the *Cambridge Archaeological Journal*. The articles are "peer-reviewed" which means that other archaeologists read and comment on the articles before final publication.

3. **Edited Volumes**—These are books written by a group of academics on a single theme, such as "Ancient Maya Warfare" or "Egypt in the Middle Kingdom." Here, each chapter is written by a different scholar about their specific project, which means the edited volume is basically a group of articles on a similar theme bound together. One scholar will act as the editor, making sure everyone else hands in their chapters in a timely manner (this can be a very difficult and time-consuming job!).

4. **A Book**—This is quite rare. Unfortunately, the academic world of archaeology bestows more "points" to professors who publish in peer-reviewed journals. Because of this situation, relatively few books on recent, cutting-edge research reach the general public. This is a major problem

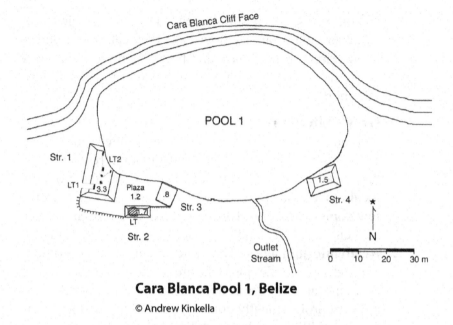

Cara Blanca Pool 1, Belize

© Andrew Kinkella

in modern archaeology and leads to the public being cut off from archaeological research and the story of the past that they deserve (see Chapter 14 for an in-depth discussion on this problem).

Example: Dr. Kinkella and the Six Steps

As a PhD student, I had to follow the six steps for my dissertation research on the ancient Maya in Belize. Step One began my first year in graduate school, where I spent the better part of a year coming up with my research questions and my overall research design. For Step Two (Set Up), I applied for a $3500.00 student research grant through the university, which I was lucky enough to receive. Part of that money was used to pay two Belizean staff members who helped me in the jungle (my "crew"). I also made a master spreadsheet recording where all my money would go, including money for lodging, airfare, car rental, a few tools, and the single most expensive thing of all, gasoline. Since I was part of a larger project, I was able to be covered by their archaeology permit, issued by the Institute of Archaeology in Belize. Step Three (Field Work) took me multiple summers, where a typical field season ran from approximately early May through late July (2.5 months). I spent my days cutting paths through the jungle, mapping Maya sites as I came across them, excavating several test pits in different Maya structures, and exploring the cenotes using both snorkeling and scuba gear.

When I got home, I began Step Four (Lab Work) where I cleaned, organized, and described the artifacts that I had found. These artifacts were mostly broken pieces of Maya pottery that I could date through seriation. I was able to make connections to other local Maya sites based on the types of pottery I found. I also made dozens of maps using all the mapping data I had collected with my compass and GPS unit. These maps showed all the structures I found, and how they related to the cenotes. I wrote up my excavation notes and made drawings of the stratigraphy I uncovered along with the locations of artifacts that I found. Lastly, I made detailed maps of the cenotes, showing their depths and describing any other characteristics that I had noted while exploring them.

Step Five was the writing of my PhD dissertation, where I brought all this information together to answer my research questions and add to the story of the past regarding how the ancient Maya used cenotes. This took me the better part of two years of constant work to write. All of the map images used throughout this book are from my dissertation. Here is the bibliographic reference:

Kinkella, Andrew. 2009. *Draw of the Sacred Water: An Archaeological Survey of the Ancient Maya Settlement at the Cara Blanca Pools, Belize.* Unpublished PhD dissertation, Riverside: Dissertation, University of California.

Finally, I published my research (Step Six) through several different outlets. I did not publish my dissertation as a book, I instead broke it up and used it to publish several different academic articles. My favorite publication is a chapter that I wrote in an edited volume called *The Archaeology of Underwater Caves.* Here is the reference:

Kinkella, Andrew, and Lisa Lucero. 2017. "Aktun Ek Nen: Reflections on the Black Mirror Cave at the Cara Blanca Pools, Belize." In *The Archaeology of Underwater Caves,* edited by Peter Campbell, 182–97. Southampton: The Highfield Press.

In the future (once this textbook is finished!), I plan to write a book about the ancient Maya cenotes of Belize for the general public.

Packing for the Trip: What to Bring on an Archaeological Project

Once our research design has been finished, our permits have been issued, and our crew is ready to go, it's time to pack for the trip! This is my checklist that I use every time I go on an archaeological project. This will tend to be specific to a jungle environment (as Belize and the Maya world is what I know best), but the requirements of most archaeological projects will be very similar. I'm assuming you've already had your required inoculations and have your needed medicines (such as hepatitis A, hepatitis B, typhoid, malaria pills, etc.). If you are working in a cold environment, you will need to add cold weather implements such as heavier jackets.

1. **The Basics**

    Passport—Do not order this last minute! Order you passport at least six weeks before you leave and alleviate last-minute anxiety.

    Airline ticket—Just don't screw this up (get to the airport on time, etc.).

    Money (cash)—Don't bother with traveler's cheques—nobody likes them.

    Credit card—ATM cards are not as good, because if they are stolen, the thief has access to your real money.

    Driver's license

    Other needed documents (e.g., dive certification, insurance card, etc.)

    Smart phone—Make sure the case is durable, and include plastic bags to store it in.

    Camera—Basic, small, and durable

    iPod and ear buds (can be part of your phone)

    Computer—An older one with sturdy carrying case (optional—not needed unless you are a grad student or above)

    Flash drive/memory stick

    Treats—Granola bars, lifesavers, whatever you like. You will be shocked how much joy can be contained in a little taste of home when you've been eating rice, beans, and tortillas for weeks. Don't skimp on this—fill empty crevices of your backpack with junk food (My old-school favorite was Jolly Ranchers).

Xerox of passport, maps—Keep one copy of your passport with you, and one at home.

Chargers and cords for electronics, and surge protector

Paperback book to read

A handful of pictures from home

A magazine or two (usually bought at the airport)

2 backpacks—One large (check) and one small (carry-on) to carry everything in.

2. **Clothes**

3 pairs pants

2 shorts

5 shirts (1 semi-nice, the rest light colored T-shirts)

6 pairs socks

6 pairs underwear

3 bandanas

Sturdy hiking boots

Tennis shoes (optional)

Flip-flops

Belt

Sunglasses

Hat

Sweatshirt—Great for the plane even if you go to a hot place. Also makes a decent pillow in tough spots.

Swimming suit

3. **Harsh Environment Survival**

2 flashlights—Ones that use AA batteries are best because you can usually find replacement batteries in many parts of the world. Odd battery sizes are not common. It's great if your second flashlight is one that can extend out into a lantern—super useful!

Clipboard—Cheap and junky are best. Don't buy one with a built-in box—it just adds clutter and weight.

Notebook (may use write-in-the-rain brand if you will be out in the rain a lot).

2 cans of bug spray—One strong, one weak. Strong one is for the day, weak one is for nighttime.

Permethrin—Spray that you put on your clothes before you go to keep bugs off. It works and can deal with several washings before it goes away (not for skin).

Sunscreen—Spray-on is best. You won't bother to put on the cream ones.

Water bottles—Holds at least two liters or more. Nalgene bottles are common here. I prefer the wide-mouth ones because you can mix Gator-aid in them much easier, but the narrow-mouth ones are much easier to drink from while driving in the back of a truck on a dirt road.

2 extra water bottles—Additional water holders. Keep ones that you buy in the airport on the way down. Buy the expensive sturdy ones with the sport tops if possible and reuse them throughout your entire trip.

Machete (usually bought once at your destination)

Trowel

Swiss Army knife

Watch

GPS (optional, but nice to have)

Compass with adjustable declination

Paperwork including many blank pieces of paper

Maps

Pencils, pens, a small ruler, drawing stuff

Gloves—Not too heavy (gardening)

Raincoat

An embarrassing amount of AA batteries

4. **Toiletries and First Aid**

Epi-pen (if you have one)

Band-aids

Bar soap

Shampoo

Deodorant

Tampons/pads/condoms, and so on

Shaving stuff

Toothbrush and toothpaste

Hairbrush

Towel (old, crappy and thin—it will dry much quicker than a new thick one)

Pills—May include malaria meds, vitamins, Pepto Bismol, Advil, Cipro

Powdered Gator-aid—A nice way to make lukewarm water tasty.

Sting-ease—You will get stung

Aloe vera—You will get burned

Q-tips

Spare plastic bags—A garbage bag or two, some gallon ziplock bags, some sandwich bags, some old grocery store plastic bags—super handy and takes up no space.

5. **Miscellaneous Tips**

Collect and horde small change.

You can always buy a spare T-shirt or two while away—no need to overpack!

Use on large and one small backpack to pack everything into—be able to carry everything you brought for a leisurely 20-minute walk by putting the large backpack on your back and the small backpack on "backwards" on your front. Don't overpack.

Don't use your phone to call people—turn off all roaming and call functions and only use it when you have Wi-Fi (FaceTime or Skype can provide the equivalent of an unlimited call for free!).

Make sure you get more than enough time stamped into your passport. If you know you will be in country for two weeks, ask for three when you enter the country. It is a huge pain to have your passport re-stamped for more time if you let it lapse.

Put pressurized bottles (bugspray, sunscreen, shaving cream, etc.) in tight plastic bags in your luggage for the flights—I have had bad luck with these things leaking while in flight.

Don't pack your trowel with your carry-on—they will take it away as a "weapon."

Guard your passport!

Send an old-fashioned letter home. The recipient will love it. It usually does take forever (weeks) to get to its destination.

This basic list has served me well for two decades of field research. Enjoy your trip—it can be life changing. And just so you know, you will get sick. While you are sick, know that you will get better (although it won't feel like it). In the next chapter, we will explore the first work that we do once we arrive at the archaeological site: survey and mapping.

CHAPTER 7

Finding and Mapping an Archaeology Site

A Bump on the Map

I had worked in the jungles of Belize for years at this point, but I was always game to try something new, especially from the comfort of my own home while I was sitting bored in front of my computer. I thought, "Hey! Why don't I pull up the Google Earth map of my survey area, and see how far I can zoom in?" I scrolled over to Belize, and then zoomed in to my research area until I couldn't zoom in anymore. The image was grainy, but it was still fun to fly across the area in a moment instead of walking across the area much more slowly and full of mosquito bites. I slowed down and started to really examine the topography. I cruised along very, very slowly with the cursor. At one point, I looked over at the altimeter. Google Earth has a feature where the elevation of the cursor is recorded by a little altimeter reading at the bottom of the page. I was rolling the cursor along the edge of a ridge, deep in the jungle. It was all the same elevation, until for a split second it wasn't.

Wait. What?

I rolled the cursor over the spot again. The elevation blipped rapidly up and down. I rolled back and forth slowly multiple times. Blip, blip, blip, blip, blip. Every time! I was pretty sure that I had just found an undiscovered Maya pyramid using Google Earth while sitting in my living room. I vowed to myself that next time I was in Belize, I would take a day and go explore that area.

Several months later, I walked out into the jungle to check it out. I found the largest single freestanding structure that I had ever found in my survey area.

Finding a Site: Survey and Mapping

Sometimes archaeology projects start at a site that has already been found, and sometimes your first job is to find the site! Here, we are going to learn how to find an archaeological site and then map it. There are only two ways to find an archaeological site. The first way is through **accidental discovery**. This is where somebody is not looking for an archaeology site at all, but accidentally stumbles right into one, which happens much more often than you think. These examples can be grand, such as Egyptian tombs found during the construction of a tourist bus roundabout in the Valley of the Kings, or more mundane like stone tools found during a hike in the mountains. Many famous finds (such as the Ice Man) were found accidentally.

The other way to find a site is through **archaeological survey**. This is a systematic plan that an archaeologist will use in order to find as many archaeological sites as they can in a given area. There are many ways to do this, but what is most important here is that the archaeologist picks a survey method that makes sense based on the research questions they are asking and the environment in which they are working. A survey for archaeological sites in the desert is much different than one done in the jungle. The size of the area surveyed must also be taken into consideration, as covering one square mile is completely different than having to cover 120 square miles. How much time you have is also a major factor.

In practice, archaeological survey is a lot of walking. You walk along the landscape and look at the ground. Are you sure you want to do this for 120 square miles, or even one square mile? I keep using the number "120 square miles" because that's how large the entire research area was when I was working on my dissertation in Belize. One hundred and twenty square miles of jungle. There was no way that I could ever walk along that entire area, staring at the ground and hoping to see some broken pieces of pottery or a small Maya house mound poking up through the jungle floor. How could I get good data without walking across the entire area?

The answer was to take a sample of the area. Since there was no way I could do it all, I chose to survey a specific piece of the land that would give me the best possibility to find archaeological sites that would relate my research design. I chose to stay near the cenotes because they were intrinsic to my research, but I had several choices on how to sample the area:

1. **Haphazard Sampling**—Just like it sounds. This is where you simply walk around the area to get a feeling for the terrain, following no set plan. This is not scientific at all, but it is easy and sometimes important archaeological finds are made when you are simply wandering around.

2. **Random Sampling**—In practice, this is one of my least favorite ways to plan a project. It is just too sciency! Sometimes, there is such thing as too much science. Here, we divide the entire survey area into equal portions. For the 120 square mile area, we could divide it into twelve, ten-square-mile portions. We then number the portions and pick three using a random number generator. We then work only in those three squares.

   You see any problems with this?

   What could go wrong here?

THINK

What if everyone knows that there is a huge site with massive pyramids in square four, but your random number generator didn't pick it? Do you just not bother with it? Yep, that's what you do. You leave it alone. I worked with a friend of mine in an area once where he attempted to do a truly random site sample. We gave up after about two days, quickly realizing that truly random samples miss one crucial component: Common sense.

3. **Stratified Sampling**—Stratified means "use of previous knowledge." Most sampling in archaeology does this. For example, if you know that sites tend to be located near water, you focus your survey on the river.

4. **Stratified Random Sampling**—This is actually a thing! Here, we are using previous knowledge (stratified), but we are also randomizing parts at the same time. To stay with the river example, we still focus our survey on the river, but we divide the river itself into squares and randomly pick a few squares

where we will do our work. This is how we can use the science of randomizing while still focusing on areas where we have a good chance of finding something.

5. **Transect**—This is a long, narrow cut through an area of a defined length and width. In my case, I did a transect through the jungle that was 400 meters wide and just over 11 kilometers long (about seven miles). Everything I found within the transect was mapped in. The transect is an excellent way to sample, as you can go between two known places (such as ancient cities) and learn about the relationship between these two places. In my case I began my transect at a Maya city named Yalbac, surveyed to the closest cenote, and then continued toward the remaining cenotes in order to explain how the cenotes related to the city.

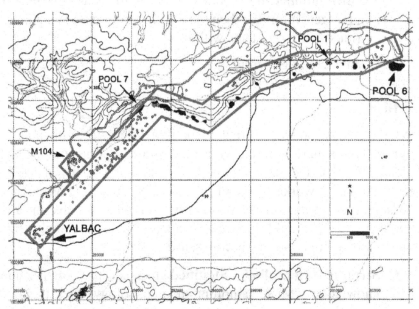

A transect in the Belizean jungle from Yalbac to the Cara Blanca Pools.

© Andrew Kinkella

Tools in Archaeology: How and What to Buy

Before we discuss the tools used in archaeological survey and mapping, I want to take a moment and give some general tips on what to look for when buying tools to take on an archaeological dig. Whenever you buy any tool for archaeological purposes, make sure that it possesses these four characteristics:

Simple—We will often ask our tools to operate at the limits of their abilities, which is why we want them to be simple. If they are simple, then they can be simply repaired when they break. Also, simple tools will tend to break less because they have fewer moving parts.

Cheap—Do not spend too much money on archaeology! Luckily for us, most of the tools we need are simple hand tools that can be had for very little money. With that said, it is sometimes worth it to spend a few dollars more to get "the good one" (especially when it comes to things like boots and compasses) but err on the side of frugality. Since everything tends to break in archaeology anyway, why not have it be something cheap instead of something expensive?

Durable—Archaeology projects put terrific strain on tools and other implements because of the dust, dirt, and general outdoor environment, so always buy the most durable version of whatever you need. Even the most durable tools will have a much shorter life expectancy than you think, especially when it comes to expensive electronic equipment.

Expendable—Finally, the tools need to be expendable. The destruction or loss of the tool should not bring your project to a halt or make you spiral into a cloud of depression. Remember this: A broken tool is not a valid reason to stop an archaeology project. It may hobble your efforts for a day, but a broken tool should be able to be either easily replaced or substituted with something else.

Specific Tools for Survey and Mapping

These are the tools that an archaeologist should have in their backpack if they are going to work on a mapping crew:

Compass—It is vital that you have a working compass with you at all times, as it will save your life if you get lost. It is also the key piece of equipment in mapmaking. You want a compass with an adjustable declination which allows you to switch to true north instead of magnetic north. That is super important! These usually cost around 60 dollars. Two common models are the Suunto MC-2 and the Silva Ranger. I prefer the Suunto by a hair, but either will do perfectly, and should last years.

GPS Unit—when I originally started teaching archaeology classes in the early 2000s, when I said "GPS" the students said, "what's that?" Now we have Global Positioning Systems (GPS) everywhere, including in our cars and in our phones. For archaeology, it's nice to get a handheld GPS unit, and you can carry it along with you as you record the area in real time. Your phone can also do an amazing amount of this kind of work, especially by downloading GPS-themed apps. Beware—your phone may not be sturdy enough to handle the rigors of archaeology and may break. Get a handheld unit, such as those made by Garmin (they usually cost around 200 dollars).

Map—Although computers and phones are full of exciting technology, nothing beats having an actual paper map of the site area out with you. If the map is too precious, then take xerox copies of the area where you work and bring several copies with you. Keep at least two in your backpack at all times in case one gets ruined! You can make notes on it, triangulate your position if necessary (using a compass), and locate yourself using the GPS points from your GPS unit.

Transit—This is an instrument reserved for the most exact calculations of distance and elevation. Only needed on very specific projects where GPS points and compass readings are not exact enough. Transits look like a mini telescope. They are used with a tripod, and have a laser built into them to take measurements down to a fraction of a millimeter. Also used with a stadia rod, which is simply a long, skinny rod with a mirror on

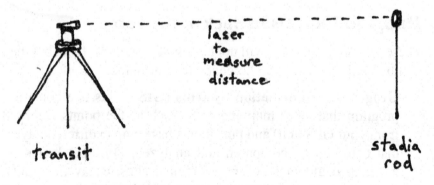

A transit and stadia rod.

© Andrew Kinkella

top. You may already have seen these being used by workmen on the side of the road as part of highway construction projects as you drive by.

Paperwork—Includes site records and extra blank sheets of paper.

Clipboard—Necessary for holding all the paperwork!

A Watch—This may seem like an odd place to list a watch, but it is vital! You must know what time it is, as the survey and mapping crew will often be in very remote areas by themselves. You need to know what time to turn around, what time to get back to the main group, and even what time to eat lunch! Do yourself a favor and buy an old-school digital watch that runs for years on the same battery—they only cost 30 bucks or so.

Pencil and Paper—I put this here so you remember to put pencils and paper in your backpack, along with a Sharpie. Why am I reminding you to put a pencil in your backpack before you hike out to a faraway site to do a day of survey and mapping? Don't ask.

Mapping Tools Used Back in the Lab

These are things that you will not have with you in the field, but they will be used in the lab later to generate your maps:

Geographic Information Systems (GIS)—this is a computer program that takes mapping data (such as the points recorded from your GPS unit) and puts it on a base map in different layers that can then be compared and analyzed. Different layers on the map could include archaeological sites, excavation units, previous excavations from years past, important geological and geographical features (like rivers and stone outcrops), and current roads. Archaeologists who learn to make GIS maps and get a GIS certificate (usually through the geography department) have a valuable skill on the job market.

Remote Sensing—This is a general category for maps that are usually produced at high altitude, away from the site (hence they are made "remotely"). Aerial photography and Google Earth maps are common here. For projects that are well funded, LiDar is an amazing tool that can make very high-resolution maps for sites covered by trees, such as in the Maya area. LiDar is done using an instrument that shoots laser light down at the ground from a plane as it flies over the area. The lasers record everything that is at the ground surface. While LiDar is very cool, it is not magic. The areas where LiDar maps are made still need to be checked out on the ground by experienced archaeological teams.

When You Make a Map

Maps are made in various scales and styles too numerous to talk about here. In general, all maps need a scale (such as one centimeter equals 10 meters), a north arrow (usually pointing to true north), a legend (where the symbols are explained), and a **datum**. The datum is of extreme importance, as it is where your map begins. All measuring begins at the datum, and it is universally marked on a map as a small triangle with a dot in the middle. It looks like this:

© Andrew Kinkella

A Typical Day of Surveying, Mapping, and Recording Sites

Every day is different on the mapping crew. On the bad days, you will walk for hours and find nothing. On the good days, your hard work will pay off and you will find archaeological sites in your survey area. Some may be large, some may be small, but the size doesn't matter as much as how you record them! Before an archaeology project begins, the archaeologist has to have a recording system in place to make all the mapping data organized and sensible. In my case, I was doing an arduous jungle transect, so whenever I came upon a structure in the jungle (no matter the size) I assigned it an "M" number and recorded its location with a GPS point. I then made a quick pace and compass map of the structure on a standardized site form, so each new structure I found got its own piece of paperwork which included its "M" number, its GPS point, and a roughly drawn map along with any other pertinent data. At larger structures, I would spend more time making the map and even possibly do some **surface collection**. Surface collection is when you collect artifacts that you see on the surface because they may yield some basic information about the site. Surface finds are not great in archaeology, as their provenience is highly suspect, and they are usually in fairly bad shape having been exposed to the elements. Still, they are very good for making a quick guess as to the site's function and age, and they also might be indicators of where to do more formal excavations in the future.

If you have been wondering what my "M" number means, the letter "M" simply stands for "mound." I found that it was a simple way to demarcate the structure numbers. If I saw "M136" in my notes, I knew that was the 136th mound or mound group that I had found on the transect, and it had an associated GPS point to locate it on a larger map. I made this organizational scheme up myself—I did not read it in a book or have it told to me by an advisor. It just seemed like a very simple way to keep things straight, and it worked great! I ended up with over 200 "M" numbered structures before my dissertation was done.

In the end, we see that the successful survey and mapping of an archaeological research area depends on first choosing a good

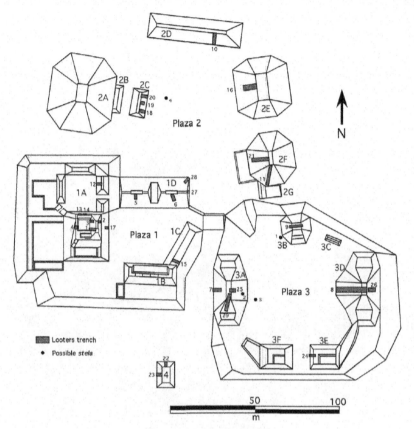

The Maya site of Yalbac.

© Andrew Kinkella

sampling strategy, and then figuring out how to implement it using the correct tools. Mapping an archaeological site or research area is usually ongoing, where the initial map is expanded and refined over the years, and new mapping methods are tried out. Once the mapping strategy is sorted out, it is time to begin excavations.

CHAPTER 8

Excavation

Destroying What We Study

In terms of digging difficulty, I would rank the soil covering an ancient Maya site in the jungle as "not that bad" to dig through. Not easy, but not too hard either. Unfortunately, this day was different. The soil that I was digging through was laughably hard, and there seemed to be no artifacts at all in the layer. I had used a trowel for the better part of a day, but I was going nowhere. As I slammed the trowel into the ground point-first to try and break up the soil, it bounced back with an audible "twang" as the steel blade bent against the solid surface then rapidly straightened again. It was like attempting to dig through a concrete driveway with a fork. I didn't want to switch to a larger digging tool because I always prefer the finesse a trowel. Big tools dig faster, but with less sense of what you are digging through. Out of options, I reluctantly switched to full-sized pick to get through the brutally hard ground. I started to swing the pick and it worked great! The ground was breaking away quickly, and I was making progress much faster than before. Oddly, as I dug, the physicality of swinging a heavy pick and slamming it into the ground brought out strong emotions in me—I had been away from home for months at that point, and I started to get sad, angry, hopeless, and lonely, all at the same time! As I swung ever harder, my emotions took over. I thought "Good god I am so tired of doing this! Why are we even digging here?" I swung harder. "There is nothing here and this is obviously worthless! I am wasting my time and I am wasting my life!" As I swung the pick down with the combined force of anger and self-pity, I heard a hollow, ringing "chink" sound that could only mean one thing. I stopped. I bent over and looked closely at the ground, knowing what I would find. As I gently swept away the hard bits of dirt with my hand, I saw what made the noise. It was a simple red potsherd with a finely carved image of a Maya man on it.

It was split perfectly into two pieces.

It was a perfect time for me to use the old archaeology joke of "Hey look! Two potsherds!" but I felt awful. "We destroy what we study" is a truism in archaeology that I first heard in my introductory archaeology class and is something that I remind myself of often. Why would I do something so stupid? In reality, there was no reasonable way that I could have kept that from happening. Even though I got overly emotional, the truth is that the area where we were digging was very tough and I had to use heavy tools. We were working very near the ground surface in an area where no artifacts had been discovered until the one I broke. In cold scientific terms, I had done nothing wrong. But I still felt like a fool.

I think of this every time I begin an excavation. Even though we "destroy what we study" in archaeology, it is our job to destroy as little as possible and get the maximum amount of information out of that which we dig up. Before we start digging, we want to be sure that we know where we are digging and why we are digging there. Digging a hole in an archaeological site with no plan is site destruction, not archaeological research. As we excavate, we want to remember that we are on a quest for information to help us tell the story of the past while keeping site destruction to a minimum. With this in mind, there are two aspects of excavation to learn: the **tools of the trade** and the **types of holes** we dig with those tools.

Personal Tools for Excavation: The Typical Collection

On a typical archaeology project, each crew member will have the items listed below. As everyone on the project will have the same tools, make sure to mark your tools by writing on them with a sharpie. I usually write my initials on them in large block letters, but feel free to get creative! Luckily, most of these required tools are very inexpensive, and you might find that you already own some of them if you clean out your closets, garages, junk drawers, and the trunk of your car. Remember the mantra of buying things for an archaeology project that we discussed in the previous chapter: Simple, cheap, durable, and expendable.

Trowel—The most important tool in archaeological excavation is the trowel. We use a mason's trowel which are diamond-shaped and flat (not the curved kind that your grandma uses in her garden). They are sturdy and inexpensive. The most famous brand of trowel is a Marshalltown. When you go on your first archaeological expedition, do yourself a favor and get a Marshalltown trowel—it will make you feel like you are in the club! Sizes vary, but one with a blade that is approximately 4.5 × 2.5 inches is probably best.

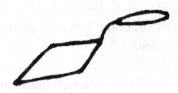

© Andrew Kinkella

3-Meter Tape Measure—We are on the Metric System in archaeology, so you need a tape measure with metric on it. In my experience, I find that 25 feet/8-meter tapes are the easiest to find. They are a bit bulky for our needs but will work fine. Make sure it has the little button that stops the tape in place (called the "stop level").

Line Level—This is a little level that you hang on a string to make sure you are holding the string perfectly flat. It is usually used to make the datum string level so depth measurements can be taken for the excavation as it progresses downward. There are plastic and metal ones—either works fine here. Pro tip—buy one that is brightly colored, as you are sure to lose it otherwise!

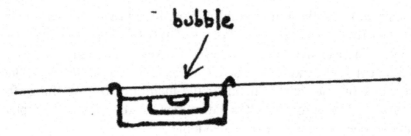

© Andrew Kinkella

Paint Brush—This should be no larger than 1.5 inches across but not less than half an inch. Any kind of bristle, whatever is cheapest. This is used for very fine excavation, which happens very rarely. At the end of the project, you will probably be the owner of a perfect condition, unused paint brush.

Whisk Broom—An old-school cane one is better than plastic. These are fantastic multipurpose tools! You can clean up your work area with them, dig with them, and use them to clean out your car after the project is over.

Clipboard—The cheaper the better. Top tip—get a large rubber band to go around the clipboard, so your papers don't flutter around on windy days.

Journal—Super important! A small notebook to write daily personal notes and musings of your experience on the archaeology project. Daily journal entries are required on most archaeology projects, as they should be! Feel free to be yourself in your journal entries and write with honesty and passion. You would be surprised at how often, years later in the lab, a single journal entry will provide the key information that unit level records, unit summaries, and photos did not.

Sharpie Pens—Black or blue—get at least two, and vary the thickness (get a fat and skinny one)

Pencils, Pens, and Paperwork—Excavation forms such as unit summary forms, unit level records, and auger records will be needed on a daily basis.

Metric Ruler—For drawing straight lines on your paperwork.

Sunscreen

Popsicle Sticks—One of the best tools for slowly digging around brittle, important finds such as human bone, as the soft wood will not damage the bone like a trowel will. Tongue depressors work great as well!

String—Needed to mark the edges of an excavation and create the datum string to measure depth.

Backpack—To keep everything in. Some people also bring a small plastic toolbox (optional).

Optional Extras

Some archaeology projects will require these things: compass, first aid kit, cotton work gloves, plumb bob, small pickaxe. I find that these are all good things to have but are often only needed sparingly.

Don't forget your lunch, your water, and some snacks!

Project Tools

These are larger, more cumbersome tools that the project will have on hand, but you are not expected to have in your own kit.

Shovels—Full-size, steel shovels. There are two common varieties, the round shovel and the flat or square shovel. This refers to the shape of the shovel blade. Round shovels are curved with a pointed end. They are great for digging shovel

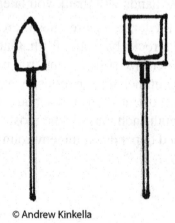

© Andrew Kinkella

test pit (STPs) or where a curved blade is needed. They are also good for "stabbing" at hard ground due to their pointy end. Flat/square shovels have a flat edge, and are great for digging when a flat, stable edge is needed such as when straightening excavation sidewalls and floors.

Small Pickaxe—These picks are small (approximately a foot long) and are great multipurpose digging tools that can also double as a hammer. They are the next step up when a trowel won't work in difficult digging conditions.

Full-sized Pick—Sometimes the dirt is so compact that even a pickaxe won't work. A full-sized, steel pick with large wooden handle will be the only thing that will get through (this is what I was using when I broke the potsherd in the story above).

Breaker Bar—A breaker bar is the worst. If you are on an excavation and someone says "get out the breaker bar" you are in for a long day. A breaker bar is a solid iron bar usually about five feet long, with one pointy end and one wedge-shaped end (it looks like a large, straight crowbar). Breaker bars are only used for the hardest, most compact soil. It works by gravity—the excavator lifts the heavy bar up perpendicular to the ground, aims either the pointy end or the wedge-shaped end at the ground (I have more luck with the wedge-shaped end), and drops it at the piece of offending soil. Progress is mind-numbingly slow, as the bar chips out little pieces of hard soil. Wear gloves! Your hands will thank you later.

Screen—This is the large, square, mesh screen held in a wooden frame that rocks back and forth. One of the rare times in archaeology where we still use imperial measurements, the screen size comes in inch designations. A half-inch mesh is quite big for archaeological purposes, and a 16th of an inch is very small. Eighth-inch mesh is the most common, but the type of screen used depends on the environment, soil type, and research design.

Buckets—Usually the common five-gallon buckets found at any hardware store. Used to move dirt, store things, and even sit on!

Tarp—Great for shade! Also used for groundcover when you want to sit down, to cover the excavation when you leave for the day, and to separate excavated material from the ground if needed. Super useful.

Munsell Soil Color Book—A book that has the official scientific color scheme used to describe soil colors. It looks like a pile of color swatches from a hardware store, but in book form.

Large Nails—Used to mark the excavation corners, and to locate the datum. You need at least five. They should be approximately a foot long.

What to Wear While Digging

Correct clothing will really increase your enjoyment of archaeology, add to your comfort, and make you safer. The first step is to dress in serviceable work-type clothing (jeans and T-shirts). Khaki pants also work fine; the tradeoff is that while khaki pants might be cooler than denim, they are not as tough. Make sure the T-shirt is thin and lightly colored. Thin long-sleeve T-shirts can also be excellent. Avoid tank tops at all costs! They do not protect your shoulders from the sun. You are going to be up and down in the dirt all day, often exposed to the sun, so your clothing really needs to be comfortable. Think in layers—whatever gives you more options is good. A small raincoat packed in the corner of your backpack can really come in handy! Make sure your boots are comfortable and in decent shape (if you have extra money, use it to buy good boots). Finally, get a wide brim hat and wear it! Baseball caps are okay, but wide brims are much better. Grandma's floppy, ugly gardening hat makes an excellent accessory for any archaeologist, because although it might destroy your budding career in fashion modelling, it will also protect your head! Let your sense of style go, and dress for comfort and protection from the elements.

Excavation Types: The Holes We Dig

Excavation types are straightforward. We will go from smallest excavation type to largest. Here, we see the tradeoff between information and destruction. The less we excavate (destroy), the less we learn, and the more we excavate (destroy), the more we learn.

1. **Auger.** An auger is a tool that is screwed into the earth to predetermined depths. It has a small bucket on the far end, usually about the size of a soda can, that is attached to a long bar. At the other end of the bar is a "T" that the digger can grab and use to screw the bucket end into the ground. On the end of the bucket are some teeth that help the bucket dig into the soil. A common way to use an auger is to screw out 10 centimeters of dirt at a time.

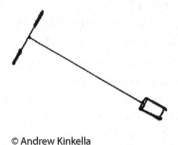

© Andrew Kinkella

Although the auger is the least invasive way to excavate a site as it moves less soil than any other method, it also gives us the least amount of data. Still, it is very good for getting a basic idea of stratigraphy under the surface before other, more invasive techniques are considered.

2. **STP.** This is a circular hole dug with a round shovel. The width of an STP varies depending on the needs of the project but is usually around 40 centimeters. Better than an auger for data collection, but still quite small.

3. **Test Pit (1 × 1 meter).** This is probably the most common excavation type in all of archaeology. Four nails are driven into the ground at each corner of a 1 × 1 meter square and then string is wrapped around the nails. The excavation then proceeds within the boundaries of the square. Once an excavation gets this big, it is often referred to as a **unit.** If you have five test pits on a site, they will likely be called Unit 1, Unit 2, and so on. A great size, as it is large enough for a person to stand or sit at the bottom and excavate. The flat sides also make it possible to see the stratigraphy as you go and note obvious soil changes and artifact densities. Also easily expandable!

4. **Expanded Test Pit (2 × 2 meter and beyond).** One very useful aspect of a 1 × 1 meter test pit is how easy it is to expand outward. You may add a second square to the side, making it a 1 × 2, and then keep going for as long as you need. I have seen excavations as large as a 5 × 5! A very organized and controllable way to excavate.

5. **Trench.** A trench is the largest excavation in archaeology. This is where a long, narrow excavation is placed across the entire site or structure. It is extremely destructive but will give us the most information of all. Because of the amount of destruction, the ability to make an excellent recording of the work is vital because the site will be very negatively impacted by all the digging, and there will be no way to get a second try. Trenches are often used when a site is about to be lost forever (such as if a dam is being constructed nearby and it will be soon underwater forever) or when a site is already in very poor shape. This type of quick, emergency archaeology is called **salvage archaeology.**

6. **Other.** Depending on the type of site an archaeologist is working at, other excavation types might be used but they are rarer. Things like tunnels into a pyramid or a 100% full

exposure of the remains of a building can be done as well, but are very complex and can be dangerous undertakings that need the specialized skillset of professional excavators, builders, and/or engineers.

Excavation: How We Dig

As with so much in archaeology, the planning and recording of an excavation must follow your research design. The questions you are attempting to answer about the past will dictate how and where you dig. Will you need to uncover lots of area? Will you need to dig deep?

There are two basic ways of uncovering an archaeological site: Excavating in a **horizontal** manner or excavating in a **vertical** manner. A horizontal excavation means that large portions of the site are being uncovered, but the digging is probably not going too deep. We do this when we want to get a snapshot of what happened at a specific time in the past over a large area. A vertical excavation tends to uncover only a small area, but the excavation goes deep. The gift of vertical excavation is the depth of the dig goes through many layers, exposing thousands of years of stratigraphy and giving us the ability to see change over time.

These examples are extremes. Most archaeological projects will do a combination of these styles of digging as they attempt to focus on a specific time period while also relating that period to what came before and what came after.

After deciding on the style of excavation and approximately how many separate units will be dug, we will then place a datum at each unit. As seen in the last chapter on mapping, the datum is the beginning point. Unlike with mapping, we will be using the datum both to locate the excavation on the map and to measure downwards from the surface as we dig. If we are digging a 1 × 1 meter unit on level ground, the datum is classically placed in the southwest corner of the unit, a few centimeters outside of the excavation itself (so you don't dig out your own datum!). A string is tied around the datum, and then the line level is used along with the measuring tape to measure how deep the hole is as excavation progresses.

As an archaeologist begins to dig down, they will have to choose how to record the layers of soil. If the layers are obvious, we will use **natural levels**. That means that the layer of dirt on the surface is level 1, and as long as the dirt maintains its same color and consistency, all artifacts found in this layer will be marked "Level 1." When the dirt changes color or consistency the digging will stop, depth measurements will be taken, a piece of paperwork called a "Unit Level Record" will be filled out, and photos will be taken of the bottom of the unit. Digging on the new layer of soil will then begin, now called "Level 2."

Doing archaeology is not hard! Let's say that the unit continues and is finally finished at Level 10. There will be 10 pieces of paperwork (unit level records) from this excavation and all the artifacts found

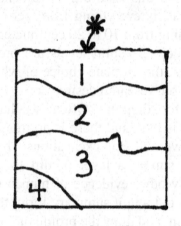

Natural Levels
© Andrew Kinkella

will be in bags labeled with the unit and the level where they are from. This is another moment when we see how important careful attention to detail is in archaeology. If the excavators mess up the recording of these levels, all is lost.

What if the stratigraphy is not obvious? What if you are digging in a unit where it's just sand the entire time with no change, or if the stratigraphy has been ruined by plowing or construction, leaving everything a big mess? In these instances, we dig in **arbitrary levels**, meaning that we assign a constant depth measurement to each level.

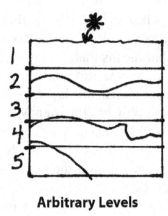

Arbitrary Levels

© Andrew Kinkella

A common way to do this is to dig in 10-centimeter levels. This means that "Level 1" is everything from zero to 10 centimeters, "Level 2" is everything from 10 to 20 centimeters, and so on.

If we have a choice, natural levels are preferred to arbitrary levels, but as always, the ultimate choice of what type of levels to dig by depends on your research design.

When do we stop digging? Often, we have to stop simply because the project is over and there is no more time to dig. If we have enough time, we will stop excavations when we reach **sterile** soil. Sterile soil is simply a layer of dirt that doesn't have any artifacts in it, or any other evidence of human occupation. At this point, we would fill out a unit summary form, take a final photo of the bottom of the unit, and draw the profile of the sidewall, showing the stratigraphy and the location of any interesting finds. The very last step is usually to **backfill** the unit. This means that after weeks of painstakingly excavating a hole with the greatest care, we grab shovels and fill it back up! Why would we do this? Backfilling a unit is smart. It keeps the area safe and secure by protecting any additional artifacts and features in the hole, by making sure that the sides of the hole won't collapse, and by making sure that no animals or humans accidentally fall in.

How to Set Up a 1 × 1 Meter Test Pit on a Typical Day

An excavation day begins when you arrive at your unit, set your backpack down, and remove the tarp that you used to cover the hole the day before. Sometimes you have problems even before you start digging—I have seen mice, frogs, snails, and snakes that have made the unit a temporary home (luckily not all at once). If you are setting up a new 1 × 1 meter unit, your day will begin like this:

1. Pick the location where you will excavate. This can be done by a grid system, such as a 1 × 1 meter unit dug every 20 meters along a north/south axis. The unit may also be dug simply where there is evidence of artifacts on the surface.
2. After the location is agreed upon, you need to take a moment and look at the ground and envision how the 1 × 1 meter unit will look once it is complete. Remember that the unit will likely be aligned to true north!
3. Put the first corner nail in. This one is easy.
4. Put the second nail in. Make sure it is aligned to true north in tandem with the first nail.
5. Put the third nail in. This is the hardest one! Measure one meter from nail #2, and 1.41 meters from nail #1. Where those two measuring tapes cross is where nail #3 goes. The specific distance of "1.41" is the square root of two. We are using the classic $a^2 + b^2 = c^2$ to get the exact diagonal measurement of

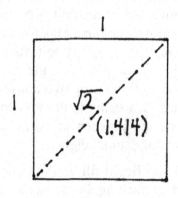

© Andrew Kinkella

the square unit ($1 + 1 = 2$, so c = the square root of two). This is important as it will give you a square with exact 90-degree corners, and not a dreaded rhombus!

6. Put the fourth nail in. Measure one meter from nail #3, and one meter from nail #1.

7. Measure the other diagonal (hypotenuse) that you did not measure yet as a test to make sure everything is perfectly square. It should also be 1.41 meters long. If it is, you are done with the nails, and are ready to string.

8. String the unit by starting at any corner and then wrapping the string to the inside of the unit, so the square is always to the inside of the nails. Think of it as if the square is floating just inside the nails.

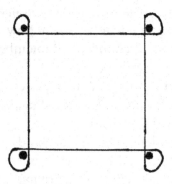

© Andrew Kinkella

9. There is one more thing to do to make the unit ready—we must set a datum stake. If the unit is on level ground, put the stake in the southwest corner. Make sure the stake is a few inches outside the square—you don't want to dig up your own datum! Bang the datum stake into the ground until it is only approximately a centimeter or two above everything else in the unit. Then attach a string to the very top of the datum and measure the distance between the string attachment and the ground. This is your datum height.

Now you are all set. Begin filling out your paperwork for the level, and then start excavating in the style agreed upon by the project (either natural or artificial levels, as described above). Go slow and stay within the lines! Keep a careful eye out for artifacts, features, and/or soil changes. When the level is done, complete your unit level record, take a photo, make a drawing, take final bottom measurements, and then begin the next level!

What If You Are Working Underwater?

Underwater archaeology has its own methods and style. Usually, these methods are generally the same as those used in on-ground archaeology, they are just adapted to work in an underwater environment. Archaeological work underwater tends to be slower, more difficult, and more expensive than on-ground, but follows the same general rules. Although the methods may be different, the underlying ideas are often the same (to tell the story of the past through artifacts). I like to say that doing archaeology underwater is like putting on a theater performance underwater—same idea, but everything goes much slower. Because of this, if you are interested in underwater archaeology, I strongly suggest that you go on an on-ground field school first. Also, take a scuba class and get your Open Water Scuba certification. If you don't like scuba diving, then you know that underwater archaeology is not for you!

The Importance of SHWA

We have gone over the tools of excavation, the styles of excavation, and how to set up a 1 × 1, but we haven't touched on the most important thing of all. To be successful in archaeology, you must have excellent **SHWA**. SHWA stands for

S = Sunscreen

H = Hat

W = Water

A = Attitude

This acronym covers the most important things you must have on any project. If you don't have sunscreen and a hat, you put yourself at major risk of getting sunburned or getting heat stroke, which puts you in danger and requires the project to stop and attend to your health needs. The same can be said for running out of water. Always bring "too much" water! A typical person working in a very hot, humid environment can drink up to one gallon of water per day. If for some reason you have extra water at the end of the day, pour it on your head to cool off! Finally, a positive attitude is vital. I don't care how strong you are, how much you've travelled, how many other projects you've been on, or how tall or short or smart or dumb you are. I need you to follow directions, do your work, make smart decisions, and work for the betterment of the entire team at the expense of your own comfort. If you are unable to work in small groups in tense situations for long periods of time, you will not be a successful archaeologist.

Ways to ruin your standing on an archaeological project:

Always eat first at meals.

Be consistently late, and always leave early.

When someone needs a quick hand, don't offer it.

Complain.

Make sure your needs are met before everyone else.

Conversely, if you can act in good faith with others, roll with the punches, be trustworthy, and give a little more than you take, I would be happy to have you on my project.

CHAPTER 9

Back in the Lab

That Achulean Hand-Axe Is Half a Million Years Old

My head was killing me. As a migraine sufferer, I found myself curled up in the back corner of the archaeology lab, laying on the carpet with my sweatshirt tied around my head. I liked the pressure that the sweatshirt gave, almost like it was fighting back the pressure coming from inside my skull. The professor who owned the lab was also a migraine sufferer and he had generously let me stay in there alone for as long as I wanted. In a fatherly way, he had made me a cup of black coffee on his way out and wished me well.

Some time went by. It was quiet in the lab.

I began to feel a bit better. It was getting late in the day, and I knew I had to start to get myself ready to leave. From my observation point curled up in a ball on the floor, I had untied the sweatshirt from my head and had been staring blankly at the storage cabinets in the lab for some time. They were the extremely nice old-school kind: dark wood, with wide, shallow drawers that were lined with crimson felt and when opened, rolled out on a whisper, perfectly balanced. As I got off the ground, I decided to look in one of the drawers. I went over and gently opened a drawer. As the drawer slid open on perfectly greased rollers, a collection of stone tools came into view. Laying on the luscious red felt were a collection of perfectly spaced Achulean Hand-Axes that had been collected from the Middle East, each with a tag recording its precise provenience. I selected one and picked it up. As I grasped it in my hand, I realized that the tool I was holding was 500,000 years old. It fit perfectly in my palm. I knew exactly how it was held because there was only one obvious way to hold it. For an instant, 500,000 years vanished, and I knew what it was like to be a *Homo erectus*. I took in the moment, then put the tool back, gently closed the drawer, and walked out of the lab. My head was feeling better.

That experience happened years ago, but I still get chills every time I think about it. The ability to have an experience like that, where half a million years melts away in a second is awe inspiring and awesome. It was made possible because my professor had carefully organized and stored his artifacts in the lab.

Into the Archaeology Lab

This is the chapter that I have feared to write. Why? Because archaeology projects come to die here. We are now in the lab work phase of archaeology. The fun and excitement of fieldwork is over. We are in the lab, spending long hours sorting shells from shell middens, weighing potsherds, measuring bones, and figuring out what kind of stone the arrowheads are made from. We are organizing our Carbon-14 samples and readying them to be sent to the specialized dating lab. We are downloading our mapping points into a geographic information system (GIS) database and plotting them on a map.

Some of this sounds fun. So why do archaeology projects come to die here? It's because these things require organized work that takes long hours and can be tedious. If you become an archaeologist, make sure you persevere through this phase. Not only is it the ethical thing to do, but I will also be very disappointed in you if you fail.

Part of what makes lab work hard in archaeology is that there are so many different ways to do it. There are different tools to use to measure, different amounts to measure and different degrees of accuracy. Here you must go back again to your initial research design. What method will be the most economical for you in terms of time and money while also giving you sufficient results? I guarantee you that whatever method you ultimately pick, no matter how rigorous and scientifically sound it is, your colleagues will tell you that you are doing it all wrong. Don't worry about them! They are just jealous that you are getting something done while they sit in the lab, immobilized by their own insecurities. Persevere through this step, and a fantastic amount of self-satisfaction awaits you!

The Lab Is Organization

The cornerstone of lab work is organization. Although organization is important in everything we do as archaeologists, it is vital when dealing with artifacts in the lab. There are all kinds of different ways to organize artifacts, and what I find is that it doesn't matter too much which way you organize things as long as you pick an organization style and stick to it. We organize artifacts based on their **attributes**. The word "attributes" is just another way of saying "characteristics," so we simply organize artifacts using their characteristics. We put these attributes into **typologies**, which is another way of saying "categories." This means that what we are doing with artifacts in the lab is simply putting them into categories based on their characteristics, but if you want to sound annoyingly full of jargon, you could say you are putting the artifacts into "typologies based on their attributes" instead of the much simpler "categories based on their characteristics." There are lots of different ways to categorize/typologize artifacts. Here are some common categories/typologies:

Chronological—Organizing artifacts based on how old they are.
Functional—Organizing artifacts based on what they were used for.
Stylistic—Organizing artifacts based on their style.
Material—Organizing artifacts based on what they are made from.

Just looking at this simple list, you can see that there are all kinds of choices for organizing artifacts from an archaeological site. If you find a ceramic bowl, you can organize it using how old it is, what it was used for, what style it is, or what type of ceramic it was made from. How do you pick which one to use? You go back to your original research design! Which typology will work best to answer the research questions that you posed? You are not forced to use only one of these. Often, artifacts will be organized under one of these overarching typologies (for instance, everything found at the site is organized by material type) but then a secondary typology will be used (once organized by material, the artifacts could be further divided up using their style). Sadly, no matter which typology you use, fellow archaeologists are sure to complain and tell you that you picked the wrong one. Don't listen to them! Pick whichever method helps with your research questions.

The Tools

The romantic world of trowels, compasses, and shovels will now give way to plastic baggies, tweezers, scales, and computers. Here is a quick list of typical tools that you will find in an archaeology lab:

Plastic baggies—Many different sizes, all acid-free.
Storage boxes—Usually typical size (like ones you use for moving), but always acid-free.
Scales—Sometimes old-style balance scales, often newer electronic "drug scale" type. To measure things in grams.
Tags—Small paper tags with lines for archaeological information pertinent to the artifacts.

Site:_____ Date:_____

UNIT#_____ QUAD: _____

LEVEL:_____cm

Feature#_____

Catalog#_____

Material:_____

TYPE:_____

Count#_____ Weight:_____

Artifact Tag.
© Andrew Kinkella

Camera with tripod/lighting—For photographing artifacts at close range.

Computers—For storing and updating the master catalog. **Microsoft Excel** and **Microsoft Access** are the most commonly used programs in the archaeology lab, and a working ability in them is always an asset. Advanced GIS programs for map making such as ArcGIS are also useful.

Trays—Used for sorting artifacts, midden, and so on. Often repurposed school or prison lunch trays.

Tweezers, dental tools, scissors, rulers, assorted pens/ pencils/sharpies—All used for the sorting of artifacts, labelling baggies/boxes, and filling out tags. Most people use whatever is comfortable. I've even seen a soup ladle used to great effect!

Shelving—Should be able to hold the collection securely and be earthquake-safe.

Mini library—Vital books on stone tool types, shell types, pottery types, and so on. These volumes are often rare and coveted, as they usually have very small publication runs and can be extremely pricey.

Sad graduate students—A handful of forlorn graduate students working on projects that seem to have no end. Bonus fun—ask them what they are working on!

A Typical Day in the Lab

A lab day starts with a goal. When you get to the lab in the morning, maybe your goal is to record 100 potsherds before you leave. Once you have your defined goal, you will take out the necessary tools and forms, and start. Make sure to take lunch! It is very important to get out of the lab, take a walk outside, get something to eat, and let your eyes focus on the horizon. Without a defined goal, you will waste time and not get anything done. The toughest task to undertake in the lab is to stay focused. As most lab work is "dull but necessary," it is all too easy to watch shows on your phone, talk with the other people in the lab, or listen to music. Don't do this! A little music is fine, but you have to force yourself to stay on task.

The "Big Three" Material Types

Most material we deal with in the lab can be divided into three basic categories: **stone**, **bone**, and **ceramics**. Although there are other materials that we encounter in the lab like metal, glass, shell, textiles, and wood, these are usually rare. I find that the "big three" are found in large quantities throughout the world, and all archaeologists should have a working knowledge in them. Below I have given you a brief primer on each, in the hopes that you will feel a little less lost than I did my first day in the lab!

Lithics: A World of Stone

The word **lithic** means stone. When archaeologists say they are doing "lithic analysis" that means they are analyzing their stone tools. Stone tools are possibly the most common artifact of all. This is because human beings have been making stone tools for millions of years, and stone is extremely durable, so it preserves when most other things won't. Before we get into types of stone tools, we want to take a moment and discuss the types of stone. Luckily there are only three general types of stone on Earth. They are

1. **Igneous**. This is stone that is created due to volcanic activity. Places where there are lots of volcanoes (like Hawaii) are made almost solely out of this type of stone. For archaeology, obsidian is the most important. Obsidian is usually dark in color and looks like glass. It is even referred to as "volcanic glass." Obsidian is a fantastic stone to make cutting implements out of, as it is sharper than steel when first made!

2. **Metamorphic**. This is stone that has been changed from its original type due to being exposed to extreme pressures within the Earth for long periods of time. In archaeology, we usually

don't deal with metamorphic stone as often as igneous and sedimentary, but there are plenty of examples, such as quartzite, which makes decent cutting tools.

3. **Sedimentary**. This is stone that has eroded over time, and then been pressed back together (by time and pressure) into something new. Sandstone is a great example of this, and often used for stone bowls and other large implements made by grinding. Oddly, chert is also sedimentary, but it doesn't look like it. Chert looks very glassy like obsidian but comes in a wide array of colors and types. Like obsidian, it is used for tools where a sharp edge is needed.

Types of Stone Tools

Stone tools can be separated into two basic categories: **chipped stone** and **ground stone**. Chipped stone tools are made by chipping away at a large core, as you "whittle" away the stone until you are satisfied with the sharp tool that you have made. The "whittling" is done by **percussion** to remove large amounts of material, and then by **pressure** near the end to do more precise, final shaping.

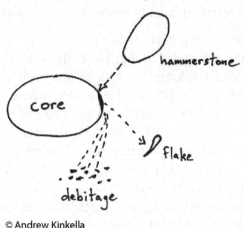

© Andrew Kinkella

Here is how chipped stone tools are made using percussion.

Here, the **hammerstone** is slammed into the **core**, and a **flake** "chips" off. There is also a lot of other miscellaneous debris that comes off at the same time that we call **debitage**. If we are making a small stone tool (like an arrowhead) we will then continue shaping the flake and keep the core for later. If we are making a big stone tool (like a spear point), we will continue knocking flakes off the core until it is shaped how we like it. Therefore, small tools tend to be "flake" tools and large tools tend to be "core" tools. Common chipped stone tools include:

Projectile points like spears, darts, and arrows—used for hunting.

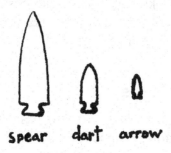

spear   dart   arrow

© Andrew Kinkella

Scrapers—Used for scraping hides.
Blades—Used for cutting.
Flakes—Simply and quickly made sharp stones used for cutting.

Some of these tools, such as the projectile points, will usually be finished using pressure flaking. Here, the roughly made tool is finished by carefully taking tiny bits of stone off the edges. This is done by using a material like deer antler, where the deer antler is pressed or "pushed" very firmly on the edge of the stone until a tiny bit of the stone breaks off. Therefore, the stone is "pushed" off by pressure, not "hit" off by percussion. You can see evidence of pressure flaking in the finely serrated edges of many tools, such as on very finely made arrowheads.

Ground stone tools are made by grinding one stone on another stone. They are smooth to the touch as they have been made by this sanding process. Most food preparation tools are made in this manner. Common ground stone tools include:

Mano and metate—Used to finely grind seeds such as corn.
The metate is the large stone slab, and the mano is the rounded

stone held in the hand that is used to grind the seeds (in Spanish, "mano" means hand).

Mortar and pestle—Used to pulverize hard, large nuts like acorns. The mortar looks like a very heavy stone bowl where the seeds are placed inside, and the pestle is a long, skinny stone (about the size of a hotdog bun) that is used to bash the seeds.

Jewelry—Things like beads and amulets, used for personal adornment.

Broken Pieces of Pottery: Ceramic Potsherds

Let's begin by getting a vital matter out of the way: the correct term is pot*sherds*, not pot*shards*. Those who say "potshards" are obviously not the type of people you want to associate with . . . In reality, we just say "sherds," as in "Hey man, are you still working on your sherds? Bummer!" Potsherds are simply broken pieces of pottery. If you drop your coffee cup, you then have potsherds. Unfortunately, it is rare to find a ceramic vessel in 100% intact shape. They are usually shattered into small pieces, most of which are missing. When we are looking at potsherds, we want to first figure out what kind of vessel the sherd was originally a part of. We can separate ceramic vessels into basic forms, which are

Plates—Broad and shallow, just like the ones you have in your cupboard.

© Andrew Kinkella

Bowls—Deep, usually with steep sides, just like the ones you have in your cupboard.

© Andrew Kinkella

Jars—Usually have the classic hourglass shape, with a narrow neck and flared opening. Can be very small or huge when used to store water or grain.

© Andrew Kinkella

Vases—Thin and straight-sided, like a simple flower vase.

© Andrew Kinkella

Figurines—I added this category because small ceramic human figurines are common in the archaeological record. They are usually broken, so be prepared to find a tiny ceramic leg, torso, or head!

© Andrew Kinkella

What about cups? In archaeology, our forms are so basic that a cup would be classified as a small bowl. Once we know the type of vessel that the sherd was from, we then measure the circumference (only a part of a vessel is needed to figure out the circumference) and try to figure out the style of that vessel. The style can give us an idea of how old the piece is, as style changes over time (remember seriation from Chapter 5?). This would be using a stylistic typology as explained above, a very common thing to do in the world of potsherds.

We would also organize our potsherds into **rims**, **bodies**, and **bases**. Rim sherds are pieces from the rim, body sherds are pieces from the body, and base sherds are from the base of the vessel. Quick thought question—which type of potsherd is the best for archaeologists to find? Is it a part of the rim, the body, or the base?

THINK

YOU CAN DO THIS!

THINK

It's the rim! I bet that some of you thought it was the body, because body sherds might have designs on them, like **polychrome** (multi-colored) imagery. That can happen, but it's rare to find. The rim gives us the most information per piece, as you can get the circumference and the form of the vessel from a rim sherd. The rim is also a spot where artistic flourishes are often done, enabling us to define style.

Working with Bones: Osteology

Most of the time, the bones found on an archaeological project are not human. You will find the remains of animals that were used for food. There are simple ways of getting great data from those bones that we will discuss in Chapter 10. For now, we can take a moment and look at human remains. Dealing with human remains is odd. It makes you think of your own mortality. It brings with it the stark realization that you are going to end up like the person you have found. No matter what you do, you are going to die. Because of the gravity of the situation, you will find yourself wanting to make jokes at the expense of the dead person. Don't do this! It is unethical and it will ultimately make you feel bad later. The reason that you want to joke is that you fear death.

If you find human remains on an archaeological project, there is usually an **osteologist** (a bone specialist) who deals with the remains. Much of their training is beyond what we need to know in an introductory archaeology textbook, and much of it even goes more into biological anthropology than archaeology. For us, I have created a short list below of how to quickly **sex** and **age** the skeleton in the field, meaning how to get an idea of how old the person was when they died, and if they were male or female. We will go down the skeleton, from top to bottom, beginning at the skull.

The Skull

Jaw line—More robust tends to be male, smoother tends to be female.

Mastoid process—A "lump" protruding downward near the ear. More robust tends to be male, smaller tends to be female.

Teeth—The more ground-down, the older the person.

Brow ridge—More robust is male, more delicate is female.

Cranial sutures—The wiggly lines that crisscross the top of the skull. The more filled in they are, the older the person is. If the skull looks totally smooth, the person is quite old.

Note—The word "**cranial**" refers to the skull, and the word "**postcranial**" refers to all the other bones in the body that aren't the skull.

The Pelvis

Overall shape—A more bowl shape tends to be female, a more angular or boxy shape tends to be male.

Public symphasis—This is at the front of the pelvis, approximately at your belt buckle. There is some cartilage there that makes a mark on the bone that changes over time. Used to guess age.

Sciatic notch—On either side of the pelvis, this is a "V" shaped notch. If it is thinner than your thumb, it's likely male. If it's wider than your thumb, it's likely female.

Other Bones

Other bones are not nearly as good for sexing and aging the skeleton as the skull and pelvis. The femur (long upper leg bone) can give you a good indication of height. The overall size of long bones can give you vague clues on sex—longer and more robust tend to be male, shorter and thinner tend to be female.

Did you notice how I said "tends to be" so often? This is because most of us have characteristics in our skeletal makeup that are not all masculine or all feminine. For example, I have a big, lumpy head. If you looked at my skull, you would be like, "Yep! That's a man!" But not so fast! Although I am tall (6-foot 1-inch), my post-cranial bones are very thin (I have very thin wrists and ankles). If you only looked at broken parts of my long bones, you might think that I was a very tall woman. To sex a skeleton, we want to examine as much of the skeleton as possible. Of course, DNA would tell us instantly the sex of the bones, but DNA tests are expensive and sometimes the bone is too weathered for DNA tests to be successful.

Don't Collect Too Many Artifacts!

Although archaeology gets its data from the collection and analysis of artifacts, we want to make sure that we don't over-collect. After the artifacts are analyzed in the lab they must be **curated**, which means stored in an organized manner for the long term. There is a **crisis in curation** in modern archaeology, which means there is not enough room to store all the stuff that we find. If you think museums want thousands of potsherds crowding up their storage space, you would be wrong. Institutions that agree to store artifacts have to sign paperwork with scary terms on it like "forever" and "in perpetuity." Storing artifacts forever is costly and complicated. This means that we must be careful and focused when we collect artifacts—we want to conduct small excavations in the right locations to find enough data to answer questions about the past, but not too much as to clog up the back rooms of universities and museums.

PART THREE

Great Themes in Archaeology

We are now at the final third of our journey. Here, we will enjoy the great themes in archaeology, current issues, and debates often over very old questions. In order, we will look at archaeology as it relates to the Environment, the Community, the Individual, the Law, the Fringe, and You.

CHAPTER 10

Archaeology and the Environment

A Pinecone in Los Angeles

Standing at the bottom of a 120-foot-deep hole looking up at the sunny skies of Southern California is disconcerting. Even though the circular hole that the construction crew dug was immense (on the order of 80 feet wide) and the sunny sky was a particularly becoming shade of blue, the feeling that the walls were forever closing in on me (reverse vertigo style) and the idea that the only way out was a flimsy metal stairway was eating away at my cool demeanor. Still, it was exciting to see the finished product after months of digging. We were way below many layers of earth that would contain the remains of human culture (that possibility would have ended after only 10 feet or so). Near the bottom, I had found what at first glance I thought was an odd piece of coal but looking closer I realized that it was a perfectly preserved pinecone made black by carbonization. I soon noticed more blackened pinecones, along with larger pieces of blackened pine tree limbs, the obvious remains of a pine forest. The deep hole had transported me tens of thousands of years into the past, to a colder, wetter time when Los Angeles had been covered by a pine forest. It is tough to take in the simple fact that the environment has changed drastically over time, and what we know as a "normal" environment for where we live is just a quick glimpse of an ever-changing world.

Reconstructing the Environment

What was it like outside thousands of years ago? Full of dry data and thankless chores, the reconstruction of the ancient environment can be seen as one of the most boring jobs in all of archaeology. The research is hard, time-consuming, exacting, and often done in the lab, far away from the daily excitement of the archaeological site. But when it is done well, the data generated from reconstructing ancient environments can be some of the most powerful and meaningful in the business. This difficult task is called **paleoenvironmental reconstruction**. Although the term is one of the longest in all of archaeology, its meaning is straightforward: "Paleo" means "old" and "reconstruction" means "to put back together," so "paleoenvironmental reconstruction" means "to put back together the old environment." Often, this data is based on **ecofacts**, which are objects in the environment like seeds and plant parts which were used by humans but not made by them. Our reconstructed environment will make it easier to figure out where people lived, as they will tend to live near resources like fresh water and good soil. We will also know what types of food they ate, and what other resources were important such as good tool stone. Ultimately, this knowledge will make it easier to find archaeological sites and understand the interplay between human culture and the environment they lived in.

How can we reconstruct the environment of hundreds or thousands of years ago? Here are some of the common artifacts and ecofacts we look at to guide us:

1. **Ice cores**—Like dendrochronology from Chapter 5, this is where we can look at layers of ice from locations in Antarctica and Greenland. These layers of ice have been added to every year over thousands of years. A core can be drilled out of them, and we can study each yearly layer as we go back in time. The ice traps things like pollen and air bubbles which we can use to reconstruct long-term global environmental trends.

2. **Plants and animals**—Plant and animal remains from the site can tell what the environment was like at the time, as certain plants and animals can only live in specific environmental conditions.
3. **Material Culture**—The artifacts from the site including tools, clothing fragments, structure remains and rock art will tell us what humans needed to survive the environment that they lived in, and what the environmental conditions were like.

A World of Dead Plants

Studying plant remains (or **flora**) is usually done by looking at ecofacts such as seeds, **pollen**, and tiny fragments of the plants themselves. If the pieces are visible to the naked eye, we call them **macrobotanical** remains. If the pieces need a microscope in order to see them, they are referred to as **microbotanical** remains. Two big problems immediately come to mind. First, how much of this is going to be preserved, and second, how do you collect tiny things like pollen from an archaeological site?

The collection of organic plant remains from an archaeological site is often done using **floatation**. Floatation uses water to separate organic material from the rocks and dirt based on the premise that organic material tends to float while non-organic material tends to sink. Here is how it works:

> A floatation "device" is simply a 55-gallon drum with a sprinkler in the bottom facing up. A hose delivers water to the sprinkler, which fills up the drum with water as it sprays upward from the bottom. When the water fills to the top, there is a lip on the edge of the drum where the water spills out. Once the drum is full of water, you need two large pieces of tulle (the web-like fabric that tutus are made out of). You put one piece under the water, and the other piece over the lip where the water spills out.
>
> Now you pour in your sample, which is soil straight from the site. The heavy rocks and dirt sink and are caught by the piece of tulle underwater (this is referred to as the **heavy fraction**). The light organic material floats and is caught in the piece of

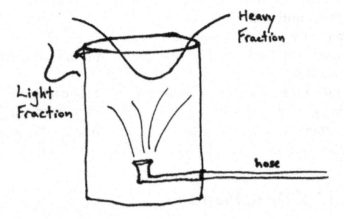

Heavy Fraction

Light Fraction

hose

© Andrew Kinkella

tulle that is covering the lip where the water spills out (this is the **light fraction**). Since the light fraction is the part that we care about, we dry it in the Sun, and then look at the sample under a microscope. It is very easy to see pollen in a microscope. Not only is it obviously different than particles of sand or soil, but it is also very particular to each plant species. This means that when you see pollen, it is very easy to tell what kind of plant it came from.

Although floatation is difficult, dirty, time-consuming work, the data we get from it is fantastic! We can say for sure what type of plants grew at the site even if no trace of them is visible to the naked eye.

A World of Dead Animals

Studying animal remains (or **fauna**) is referred to as **zooarchaeology** or **faunal analysis**. This is usually where specialists study the animal bones from an archaeological site to try and make sense out of the ancient environment and the diet of the people who lived in it. Besides bones, they may also study **coprolites**, which is ancient human poo. Coprolite study is rare, because it is hard to find ancient human poo in the archaeological record, but even though the research sounds disgusting and anyone who does it is required to be the brunt of a thousand shitty jokes (ha!), the data on ancient diet that comes from this is excellent.

In my experience, the broken animal bones found at an archaeology site tend to be in a sorry state. Broken into tiny pieces less than an inch long, most of them can't be typed any further than the basic "mammal" or "bird." Sometimes you can tell that they have been cooked (they looked burned or very shiny). Even when we can figure out the species of the bone fragment, then what? Can we say something more meaningful about the animals that are related to the site beyond, "hey look, it's a rabbit?"

If I simply count up the total number of rabbit bones found at the site, that does not tell me much. Let's say that I have 106 rabbit bone fragments. I have a number, but I can't really compare it to anything in a meaningful way. If I was to break all the bones in half, then I would have 212 rabbit bones. The number does not have meaning. In order to get a meaningful number of bones, one of my favorite things to do with bone is to run a **minimum number of individuals (MNI)** calculation. Here, we will figure out the minimum number of rabbits that had to die to provide the bones found at the site. We do this by counting specific bones. If I find 19 pelvises, 11 right-rear leg bones, and 26 skulls, the minimum number of rabbits that had to die to make this collection is 26. Although there are definitely more dead rabbits in this collection than 26, I can prove 26 for sure. With this number, we can then compare the MNI to other animals at the site like deer or fish and begin to make real conclusions about how much hunting was going on per animal, and how plentiful the animals were in the environment at the time. MNI enables us to get meaningful numbers from some very basic remains.

Rock Art Tells So Much and So Little

One of the best ways to get information on ancient environment is to look for drawings of it from the past! People of the past drew their world and their environment just like we do. If we are lucky enough to work in an area that has preserved **rock art**, there is a chance that we have proof of what the environment was like based on the images. For example, if you aren't sure if antelope lived in the area at the time, but you find an image carved in stone of an antelope running, there you go! Rock art is a fantastic archaeological resource.

Rock art gets much more difficult to translate if people of the past were using it symbolically. If we find an image of an antelope like in the example above, we can all agree on the overwhelming evidence that the image gives for the existence of antelope. What if the rock art consists of lines and dots, or stick figures, or circles and handprints? There is no way to truly know what these images mean, as they are symbolic representations of ideas that were in the head of the artist. Even when the meaning of the art may elude us, we can still record the basic styles of the rock art:

Pictographs—Rock art done using paint.

Petroglyphs—Rock art that is carved into the stone.

Cupules—Shallow, smooth, circular carved depressions (about the size of the bottom of a Coke can) that are carved into important boulders and locations. Can be by themselves, in lines, or many together.

Geoglyphs—Large (many acres in size) images made on the ground. The Nazca Lines are the most famous example.

Important Environmental Trends

Sometimes archaeology gives us information that goes well beyond the discipline and toward our general knowledge of life on Earth. Although we can look to geology for extremely long-term environmental trends, two of the most important environmental changes for modern humans took place in the recent past:

1. **The Medieval Warm Period**—This lasted from approximately 800–1300 AD, where climate was generally a bit warmer and dryer.
2. **The Little Ice Age**—From approximately 1300–1850 AD, where climate gets a bit colder and wetter.

These changes small (on the order of a few degrees) and are well-documented, but they would have not affected all areas of the Earth equally. Also, we must remember that not all human trends can be explained by only environmental changes. Still, it is interesting to note that the ancient Maya collapse happened at approximately 850

AD (as things got hotter and dryer, creating major droughts), and the Vikings experienced major problems at around 1300 AD (when climate got colder, making boat travel in the North Atlantic much more difficult).

A Last Look at the Environment

Remember the Lorax quote, "Unless somebody cares a whole awful lot, nothing is going to get better. It's not." This is the future of both archaeology and the environment. Practically every archaeologist I know becomes more and more of an environmentalist as time goes on. As the years go by, they see the environment around their archaeological site denuded of trees, ravaged by fires, disrespected by other people, or ruined by development. It is supremely disheartening.

Examples of Ancient Environmental Changes

Easter Island—The Island of Rapa Nui (Easter Island) is located in the middle of the Pacific, thousands of miles away from everybody else. The story of the people who are famous for constructing the large stone statues (Moai) is one of difficult choices based on long-term environmental changes and shortages.

The Vikings—The rise and fall of the Vikings mirrored the Medieval Warm Period and the Little Ice Age. They Vikings expanded across the Atlantic during the Medieval Warm Period, and then the colder temperatures of the Little Ice Age reversed their progress.

CHAPTER 11

Archaeology and the Village

Las Vegas Is Stupid

Looking out upon the Nevada desert from a commanding view inside the Luxor, I was overwhelmed with a singular idea: Las Vegas is stupid. Why would human beings make a huge city in the middle of the desert with little water, scarce resources for crops (such as fertile soil), and far away from major rivers for water, transportation, and trade? If we think of modern examples of settlements, we can begin to see some interesting and strange choices that our society has made. Why is Las Vegas in the middle of a desert? From the purely environmental view that we talked about in the previous chapter, Las Vegas is in a terrible spot. Why put it there?

We know Las Vegas is located where it is because of state laws that allow gambling. Although it makes little sense from an environmental standpoint, it makes perfect sense from a cultural standpoint and more specifically an economic standpoint. People of the past will have their own examples of a "Las Vegas," where the location of their villages and cities may make no sense to us initially. Just like archaeologists of the future will have a terrible time figuring out why Las Vegas is located in such a strange spot, it is up to us to figure out the underlying reasoning for the location of archaeological sites.

Location, Location, Location

The idea of location is central to this chapter. We are attempting to answer questions about how and why people chose to live in particular places, what types of communities grew there, and what happened in those specific places while people lived there. Looking at location can answer questions such as:

"Were the ancient people of this village part of a larger city center?"

"Did the people of this village farm?"

"How important was trade?"

"Did warfare play a large role in village life?"

"Were there areas that were considered sacred?"

As we look at the remains of an ancient settlement, the unit of measurement is the **house**. In archaeology, the word "house" is usually combined with other words, but they all mean basically the same thing. You may encounter:

A **house mound**—The remains of an ancient house.

Household groups—Several structures found together, often with a **plaza** in between them (also called "Plazuela groups").

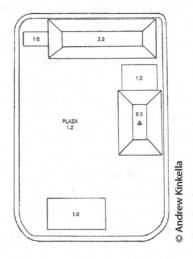

Household archaeology—Archaeology that focuses on the household level, as opposed to focusing on large pyramids and huge sites. This type of research will also focus on "**commoners**" (everyday people) as opposed to the **elite** class (kings and queens).

When we focus on the remains of a house, we are hoping to define **activity areas**. Activity areas are the specific spots in the house where specific activities happened, like a kitchen or bedroom. When looking at the remains of an ancient house, the kitchen area is usually the easiest one to spot. Why do you think the kitchen area is the easiest to find?

THINK

It's because there are so many artifacts associated with preparing food! Groundstone for grinding seeds, sharp stone tools for cutting, a hearth for cooking the food, and leftover animal bones from eating. All of these artifacts and features are durable and easily defined in the archaeological record. There may also be other activity areas that can be found nearby, like stone tool production areas (will have lots of broken stone bits leftover where they made and sharpened tools) or a midden (where garbage was thrown out).

Household archaeology sounds boring because it is not dealing with huge pyramids and lavish burials. If there is a choice between working on a big pyramid and working on house mounds on an archaeology project, my students will always pick the big pyramid first. As the weeks go by, that choice changes. Students realize that the chances of finding the golden tomb of a long-dead king inside a pyramid are tiny, whereas the chances of finding interesting artifacts in a house mound is quite good! By the end of the season, there are plenty of volunteers to work on the house mounds, while interest in working on the "big pyramid" wanes.

Understanding the "Why" of Location

Why did they choose to live there? Sometimes that question is easy to answer, like when a village is next to water, but sometimes it is hard, like in the Las Vegas example above. The study of how human beings spread themselves out over the landscape is called **settlement pattern** analysis. When we look at settlement patterns, we can learn all kinds of things about an ancient society without doing any digging at all! We simply look at the location of the mapped sites. The survey and mapping data collected with GPS, LiDar, and other mapping equipment is extremely important here. As we look at the general area where the village is located, we can start to incorporate the surrounding environment. We can walk out beyond the village and start recording the features of the natural world that relate to the village, like rivers, forests, and good soils for growing crops. We can do a **site catchment analysis**, which is an educated guess about how many people the local environment could support based on food and water needs. This leads us to estimates of **population**.

How many people used to live here? This is a very common question in archaeology. We are all curious about how many people lived in a place that is now desolate and overgrown. Population numbers are classically hard to guess at, because so many variables go into the total number. How many people lived in each house? How many houses were in existence in the village at any one time? Are all the mounds that we see houses, or are some of them workshops? If you hear a population number given for an archaeological site, chances are that the published number is a bit higher than the reality, as all of the variables that I just listed tend to lower the total number. Realize that although the population number guessed at by an archaeologist is likely nowhere near exact, this is a question we get all the time and we are doing our best to answer something that is very difficult to know.

Evidence for **trade** is more straightforward. If we are working at a village and find something that is not local, guess how it got there? Trade. Common trade goods are things like good-quality stone for making stone tools and special ceramics that are not made locally. Nonlocal stone is a fantastic thing to find archaeologically, because the stone can be **sourced** to the outcrop where it came from. Ceramics can also be sourced to where the clay was from, and nonlocal animal bones and plant materials can be sourced to where they are native. Using this data, trade relations between settlements can be defined and trade networks can be traced.

The Idea of Landscape in Archaeology

We can use the location of the village to get still more hints on how the people of the past viewed their environment. We can look at the overall settlement **landscape.** In archaeology, we use the word "landscape" in a very specific way. We say that "landscape" is the *perception* of the environment, as created by humans. Notice that I have underlined the word "perception." This is because in archaeology, landscape refers to how we as humans perceive our everyday environment, which goes beyond straight facts and into the realm of the mind and belief.

Yosemite National Park is a great example of landscape in action. Why don't more people live there? It is a very large area with plenty of water and tons of trees that could be cut down and used to make houses, yet very few people live there. Yosemite is like Las Vegas in reverse! This will be very confusing for archaeologists of the future. They will say, "It seems like the perfect place for a large settlement, yet barely anybody lived there. Why?"

Because it's pretty.

We have decided in our society to set aside areas that we *perceive* to have incredible natural beauty, for the enjoyment of all citizens. We define the landscape of Yosemite as "pretty." Human beings do not just follow strict environmental facts when they decide where to live, they follow their beliefs and experiences as well. People of the past had special areas just like us, places of special meaning. We refer to these spaces as **sacred space** or **ritual space**. In archaeological terms, we would define Yosemite as sacred space. Archaeology of the village is so much more than just the village itself. Not only do we explore the houses and activity areas within the village, but we also take into account the relationship of the village to other villages, to the surrounding environment, and to the beliefs of the people who once lived there.

Example of a Village

There are innumerable examples of ancient villages located across the globe. For our example, we could narrow it down to the North American continent, where Native American villages all have different settlement patterns based on a mix of different environmental resources and different cultural perceptions of the landscape. We could look to the southern coast of **California**, where the largest **Chumash** villages housed approximately 700 people, and were located where freshwater streams emptied into the Pacific Ocean. This location gave them maximum access to resources: fresh water from the stream, fish and shellfish from the ocean, deer and other animals from the land, and acorns from the oak tree groves nearby. Other resources were obtained through large trade networks, including trade with the California Channel Islands using a plank canoe called a tomol. The Chumash also had sacred spaces, such as important geographic spots on the landscape (like mountain tops and promontories overlooking the beach), cemeteries, and rock art sites. Even within Chumash territory, different villages will have different life histories based on a mix between environmental variation and human choice. By studying settlement patterns and landscape as it relates to Chumash villages, we can give compelling answers to "why did they live there?" as we continue to tell the story of the past.

CHAPTER 12

Archaeology and the Individual

A Singular Person

"I'm going to be just like him someday. Dead." I was sitting at the side of an excavation unit at an ancient Maya city in Belize, looking at the remains of an individual that was well over a thousand years old. His skeleton was very well preserved in the jungle soil, and the crew had done an excellent job of exposing the entire skeleton at the bottom of the pit. The crew was off eating lunch, and I was alone with him. I stared at the skeleton for a while, and I thought about death. I thought about how I would never know this person's name, and in thousands of years nobody will probably know my name. I thought about how I could move around, and he could not. It was so odd to think that this skeleton used to have skin and a name and could breathe and walk. I thought about how he would have had parents, and probably had a wife and kids. Maybe some of his descendants were still alive. Looking closely at his skull, I felt bad that there was a tree root growing through the side of it. The tree root looked very painful, which was silly of me to think because the root grew through his skull over a thousand years after his death. Still, it bothered me.

The Individual

If I ask you to name a famous individual from history, you will probably come up with people like Abraham Lincoln, Gloria Steinem, or even King Tut. Since these people were incredibly famous during their life, reconstructing facts about their life seems like it would not be too hard. Attempting to reconstruct the identity of a particular individual who may have lived thousands of years ago is brutally difficult. Most people of the past are nameless individuals to us. We must remember that each of them had a name, a mom, a dad, and likes and dislikes. Remembering how human this person once was helps us treat their remains in an ethical manner.

Working on human remains always makes me very introspective. I think of my own mortality, and how the person I am working with would have wanted to still be alive. I think they would probably like that we were talking about them, even though we don't know their name.

How do we figure out the identity of a specific person from the past? Identity can refer to many aspects of a person's being. I like to split up the study of a singular person into two broad categories. Category one is what I call the "data of the dead" which are the basic data of the individual that is found at the archaeological site. Category two is the "identity of the dead" where the data found at the site is analyzed and we start to figure out the facts of this person's life.

The Data of the Dead

When looking at the remains of a person found at an archaeological site, we will record the following:

1. **Body**—This is the actual body itself, which is usually human bones in fairly poor condition. When we encounter human remains, we will either leave them in place or collect the remains for further study in the lab. Work on human remains progresses very slowly, with tools like dental tools and popsicle sticks used in the excavation. The human remains are the single most important thing to study when we are trying to reconstruct the life of the individual, as the bones can tell us about age, health, DNA relationships, and cause of death.

2. **Associated artifacts**—These are the artifacts that are associated with the burial. These artifacts can be things like beads, ceramics, stone tools, and possibly pieces of clothing like buttons.

3. **Location and position**—While we record the body, we will note precisely where and how the body was buried. The location (such as in the middle of a pyramid) will be recorded as will the position of the body (such as laying prone or in a fetal position). The body may also be pointing to one of the cardinal directions, and be buried either alone or with multiple individuals.

4. **Written records**—On rare occasions, we will have written records to consult such as a government document or headstone. Sometimes, a hieroglyphic passage or a piece of art depicting the individual in life may be found, but this is extremely rare.

5. **Other**—Other studies such as environmental and/or ethnographic research may be consulted to relate the person to their larger culture area.

Identity of the Dead

Once the initial recording of an individual's remains has been completed, we move into the analysis phase. Here, we are using our data to describe the life of the individual. There are many different ways that this analysis can go based on the amount and quality of the data that we have.

1. **"The Biological Facts"**

   This is my catch-all category for the typical biological traits of the person. These are the types of traits that you would find on a driver's license, such as height, weight, and eye color. We can also record other biological data that is found on the individual's remains and in their DNA. For example, we may record any diseases (such as arthritis) that we notice as we study the skeleton. From this list, you can see that some of these facts are much easier to find than others. Depending on the condition of the remains, we may never know some of these things (such as eye color).

2. **Social Ranking, Status, and Class**

For social ranking and class, we are trying to define if the person was a "commoner" (everyday person) or an "elite" (person of social stature, such as a king or queen). Social ranking can be guessed at based on the associated artifacts found with the body. Lots of expensive artifacts would indicate high status, whereas no artifacts would indicate low status. Status may also be inferred by the location of the burial. If the burial is located in an ornate chamber in the middle of a pyramid, the individual is a high-status person. We may also be able to tell if they had a job that came with social stature based on specific artifacts found in with the burial. For instance, if the person is buried with lots religious iconography, they may have been a religious figure of stature. These examples show how difficult it usually is to infer specifics about social ranking beyond "they look rich" and "they look poor."

3. **Gender (Roles)**

When I discuss gender here, I mean the cultural component of our identity as opposed to our biology. We can begin to define the varied social roles of males and females within the society based on their grave goods. Men will be buried with artifacts that may point to specific male gender roles they had in life, whereas females will be buried with artifacts that point to female gender roles. Examples of gender roles include jobs and chores, things like hunter, cook, farmer, carpenter, or religious leader. Sometimes, the gender role differences between men and women will be very strict, whereas at other times, they will be more muted. Some social roles are not gendered, meaning either of the sexes can do them. In rare cases, we may see biological males exhibiting female gender roles (or the other way around), which may point to a defined third gender in the society.

Some societies have a defined third gender (such as the berdache in certain Native American societies, which is a male who takes on specific female roles) and some do not. We have to remember to not let our own notions of gender roles get in the way of the archaeology, and let the data speak for itself. For instance, just because we think of a hunter as a classically male role, that does not mean that a hunter is male in all societies.

4. **Ideas, Beliefs, Religion, and Ideology**

We ultimately hope to reconstruct what this person thought and believed when they were alive. What was their religion? What types of rituals were they involved in? If we happen to find a religious amulet with the dead person, then that can point us toward their religious beliefs. A headstone would also help in this instance. Unfortunately, finds like that are extremely rare. How do you reconstruct the belief system of the person if all you have is the body? The location of the burial may give clues (for example, if the burial was in a special, meaningful location). Something as simple as the direction the head is pointed in (for example, the burial is aligned to the rising sun in the east) may also allude to religious belief. The ideology of the dead person (what they thought and believed) can be extremely difficult to reconstruct. These ideas are often guessed at based on knowledge we have of the larger culture that the dead person belonged to rather than any specific artifacts found with the burial. We may also guess at past beliefs using general anthropological theory, such as how rituals work in all human societies (remember our discussions on reconstructing a birthday party from Chapter 3).

As we list all the traits that we would like to reconstruct about the life of the dead individual, you can begin to have an appreciation for how difficult most of these things are to figure out. We also see that the preservation and overall condition of the burial will make a massive difference in how much we can ultimately reconstruct about the life history of a particular person.

Ethics

What is the right thing to do when we are excavating the dead? How do we act in good faith with those who are long dead, as well as with their current families or communities? Is it right to dig up the dead in the first place? Ethics are a major concern in archaeology. We want to do the right thing for the present and the past. We want to be ethical with excavating artifacts and also when storing them. Sometimes, it helps to simply listen to the little voice inside your head. If you feel like what you are doing is a bit unethical, it probably is. Being ethical does not mean halting all archaeological work, as it is only through archaeology that we can learn about certain aspects of the past. Our job is to find balance between ethical behavior and the pursuit of scientific knowledge. In the next Chapter 13, we will attempt to put some parameters on what it means to do the right thing in archaeology. We will explore archaeology and the law.

Examples of Individuals in Archaeology:

King Tutankhamun—Famous New Kingdom pharaoh from the 1300s BC in Egypt (see Chapter 2).

Kennewick Man—9000-year-old Native American burial found in Washington State (see Chapter 13).

John Torrington, the Frozen Man—A crewmember on the ill-fated Franklin expedition who died in 1847 and was buried in the permafrost on Beechey Island in far Northern Canada.

Otzi the Ice Man—5,300-year-old frozen man found in the Italian Alps in 1991 (see Chapter 4).

Pacal the Great—Maya King from the Classic Period (seventh century AD) found in a tomb at the site of Palenque.

CHAPTER 13

Archaeology and the Law

Stopping the Developers

I had not seen any artifact of any kind in weeks. As the archaeological monitor for a major water system renovation project in downtown Los Angeles, the fact that I had found nothing made me happy. As I watched the construction crews dig massive holes with backhoes and drills, I silently rejoiced that I did not have to stop the project. Everyone thinks that archaeologists always want to find something, but sometimes we don't. I thought about this as I watched the drill pull another load of dirt out of the ground and watched a large, smooth stone fall at my feet.

Wait. Oh no…

Picking up the stone, I immediately recognized the perfectly smooth side. It was a mano—a tool that would have been used by Native Americans to grind seeds. I sighed, then raised my hand and made a fist, the universal construction sign meaning "STOP!" The operator stopped digging, got out of his machine, and gave me the biggest barrage of name calling, shouting and swearing that I have ever experienced in my life. He was shouting "That's just a rock! That's nothing!" As he shouted, I called the foreman over. I showed him the artifact and told him I would have to shut down construction in a 50-foot circle around the find. The foreman understood and told the drill operator it wasn't his fault. I agreed. The drill operator told me he was sorry. I totally understood. In construction, everything is about speed. If you are slow on your job, you can be replaced.

The next day I met with the land developer, who immediately tried to blame me for the fact that they were 50 days behind schedule. Even though my little 50-foot circle had only been created the day before and was a minuscule part of their multi-acre development that spanned several city blocks in downtown Los Angeles, I was somehow the cause of their slowness. I told him that was ludicrous, and he backed down. The next day, myself, a Native American Monitor, and several other archaeologists allowed the excavations in the 50-foot circle to continue, but at a slow pace so we could see if any additional artifacts came up. We watched closely for the next week and did some quick test excavations, but we never found any other artifacts. Finding nothing, we let the development continue at full speed.

The job of archaeology is not to stop development. We must remember that people need houses, development does need to happen, and that if we as archaeologists find no evidence of human life in the soil, we cannot stop development from occurring and it would not be ethical for us to do so. In this chapter, we explore the law and how it relates to the job of telling the story of the past through the artifacts that we find.

Laws in Archaeology

Today, there are many laws that both protect archaeological sites and affect our abilities to practice archaeology. We will discuss the three that are the most significant. It is important to note that these laws only affect archaeology in the United States. Each country has its own laws, so archaeological sites are protected (or not) in many different ways throughout the world. The three laws that we will look at are:

1. **The Antiquities Act of 1906**
2. **The National Historic Preservation Act (NHPA) of 1966**
3. **The Native American Graves Protection and Repatriation Act (NAGPRA) of 1990**

These laws help us answer the question, "Who owns the past?" It seems like nobody and everybody owns the past at the same time. Although this question is often philosophical, there are times when we need a definitive answer. In my experience, there is no consistent answer to this question—it depends on the circumstance. Possible owners of the past include:

- Descendants/the family related to the artifacts.
- The culture related to the artifacts.
- The government of the country where the artifacts are found.
- The landowner that owns the land where the artifacts are found.
- Everyone?

Since the question of "Who owns the past?" can be so difficult, we must look to the laws in place to give us guidance.

The Antiquities Act of 1906

This is the very first law protecting archaeological sites in the United States. This legislation was created because some of the famous Native sites in the American Southwest (such as Mesa Verde) were being brutalized and destroyed by looters. People from other countries could also come to the United States, excavate artifacts, and take them out of the country for good. The Antiquities Act was enacted to combat these situations. It gave the president (Teddy Roosevelt at the time) the ability to designate specific parcels of land as "National Monuments." The Antiquities Act did not protect all archaeological sites in America, just the ones that were on the protected National Monument land in each specific case. Still, this law was an important step forward to bringing the protection of archaeological sites into conversations at the national level.

The National Historic Preservation Act (NHPA) of 1966

For archaeology, this is the most important law of them all. Although NAGPRA is more famous (see below), the NHPA gave America a framework for dealing with all archaeological sites in the country at a federal level. What began as an effort to save the downtowns of America from destruction due to new freeway and suburb construction of the 1950s became organized, far-reaching legislation that created an entire new branch of archaeology.

The NHPA states that any construction undertaken on federal land or using federal money (which is most large construction projects) needs to be checked out for "**cultural resources**" before the project can go forward. Cultural resources are any material remains from our shared American history, including artifacts from Native American history as well as from early American history (such as from the Civil War). This would also include entire archaeological sites as well as historic buildings and homes. The specific portion of the law that requires this oversight is called "**Section 106**," so archaeologists will often talk about "the Section 106 process" without ever mentioning the NHPA by name (it is understood).

To protect these resources, the NHPA created the office of the **State Historic Preservation Officer (SHPO)**. Every state in America has a SHPO, and this person oversees the protection of these sites in their state. The NHPA also created a master list of important historic places, called the **National Register of Historic Places**. These places are protected from development. In order to get an archaeological site on the National Register, it must fulfill one of the following four categories (I have added an example as well):

A. **Made by a master.** A historic home made by a famous architect like Frank Lloyd Wright.

B. **Relates to a famous person or event.** George Washington's house at Mount Vernon.

C. **Part of a famous style or movement.** The Victorian style homes of the late nineteenth century.

D. **May add to our knowledge of history at some point in the future.** A catch-all category that includes virtually every archaeological site ever.

Category "D" seems like cheating. Won't just about any historic home or archaeological site add to our knowledge of history at some point in the future? The answer is yes, but there is one important aspect of the NHPA that renders this point moot. All archaeological sites up for National Register consideration must be argued for in terms of **significance**. Only the best of the best are chosen for protection. Just because George Washington touched a house one time does not make it eligible for National Register protection. The idea of significance is hugely important when it comes to archaeological law. Often, it is the archaeologist in the field who decides the fate of a site by deciding on its significance.

The NHPA did one more extremely important thing for archaeology. It created an entirely new branch of the discipline! Due to the need for archaeologists to now check out all development on federal lands, **cultural resource management (CRM)** archaeology was born. This is often referred to as "archaeology for hire." Unlike classic academic archaeology, a CRM archaeologist works for a firm (like a lawyer). The firm will send the archaeologist out on specific jobs to monitor the initial construction phases of large development projects, to watch the digging to make sure artifacts or burials are not disturbed. If the archaeologist finds artifacts (also called "cultural resources"), they must stop the development project and come up with a plan to save the archaeological site by either having the developer move to another area (this almost never happens) or having the developer pay for a full-scale archaeology project to record the site. Due to the cost of paying for a full-scale archaeology project, developers never want to find archaeological sites. CRM archaeology is the number one employer of archaeologists in the United States (see Chapter 15).

The Native American Graves Protection and Repatriation Act (NAGPRA) of 1990

This law gives Native American communities power to say what will happen to the remains of their ancestors. NAGPRA is specifically focused on Native American burial remains and the associated artifacts from burials but is sometimes implemented when any artifacts or sites of deep tribal importance are uncovered. Some of my students have trouble with the word "repatriation," which simply means "to give back." What the law is telling us is that we must protect the graves and give them back. If an archaeologist finds a Native American grave, they must stop digging immediately and reach out to the local tribe for guidance on how to proceed.

When the NAGPRA process goes into effect, a **Native American monitor** who will come out to the archaeological project and watch the excavations. This person is a member of the local tribe. They will talk with the archaeologist about how the project will proceed, and the two of them work together on the plan going forward. The monitor has the final say on how any burial material is handled. They may want the burial excavated and moved elsewhere or left in place exactly as it was found. They may want further study (such as Carbon-14 dates) or they may want nothing else to happen. The archaeologist complies with whatever the monitor says.

Sometimes, the media makes it seem like archaeologists and the Native American community are on opposite sides of the spectrum, constantly battling for ownership of the past. Although there are extreme examples of this, the vast majority of interactions between archaeologists and Native people are very positive. I enjoy working with a Native American monitor, as both of us are focused on the same thing—telling the story of the past and making sure the remains are handled with dignity and respect.

Examples of Archaeology and the Law

These three examples illustrate how modern archaeology laws have preserved our shared cultural heritage. Without the law, all of these archaeological treasures (and thousands more) would be lost forever.

1. **Mesa Verde**—Amazing cliff dwelling in Arizona, saved due to the use of the Antiquities Act by Teddy Roosevelt.
2. **The Slave Burial Ground**—An accidental find in Manhattan in the 1990s, this is a burial ground for African American slaves used throughout the eighteenth century. 360 burials were uncovered, 10,000–20,000 are estimated to still be underground. Saved due to the NHPA.
3. **Kennewick Man**—A 9,000-year-old burial found in Washington State in the 1990s. As one of he oldest human burials ever found in the New World, there was much archaeological interest in this find. Famous for the arguing between archaeologists and the Native community, Kennewick Man was ultimately studied by archaeologists and handed over to the Native tribe, following NAGPRA.

CHAPTER 14

Archaeology, the Media, and the Fringe

Cold in the Tomb

Back in 1993, during my first field season in Belize, I was working in a Maya tomb. The tomb had been looted, so most of the human remains and artifacts were gone. It was my job to draw a map of the tomb by measuring its dimensions, and record any other artifacts still present inside. The tomb was located near the top of the largest pyramid at the site, and the only way in was to crawl through a tight, dangerous looter's hole. Luckily, hole was only a few feet long, so I pushed my backpack through, and then crawled in with my flashlight in my teeth. Inside, the tomb was tiny, about three-feet tall, three-feet wide, and six-feet long. I was cramped as I sat in a low crouch, took out my clipboard and measuring tape, and started taking measurements. The work was going fine, but the inside of the tomb was stiflingly hot. As I measured, sweat poured off my forehead and onto my papers. Undaunted and wanting to finish, I recorded the remaining measurements and checked the floor of the tomb for any artifacts to record. Unfortunately, the looters had been very meticulous in their thievery, and there was nothing to add to the paperwork. As I put my tools back in my backpack, I was suddenly overcome with a feeling of extreme, overwhelming cold. I dropped my backpack and shivered uncontrollably for several seconds. And then just as it began, it was mysteriously gone . . .

What happened to me? Did the soul of the long-dead Maya king flow through my body, warning me to leave or be cursed for all eternity? Had I disturbed one dead soul too many? Was I marked for death by the world of the beyond? I could easily pepper this story with false feelings and fake stories, making connections that are not there, and sell it to an unsuspecting audience. In reality, I was probably a little dehydrated, had sweated too much, and my body over-cooled itself for a few seconds. But you do not want to hear that, because it is straightforward, factual, and uninteresting. You want the dead Maya soul to flow through my body, because it is much more satisfying! The problem with the dead Maya king scenario is that none of it is supported by data or evidence.

Welcome to the Fringe

It is this kind of thinking that brings us to the world of archaeology and the fringe. Also referred to as **pseudoarchaeology** or **pseudoscience**, people who sell these stories take unsubstantiated, silly stories like the one above and tweak them into great soundbites. We must be very wary of the fringe. The fringe makes up stories that are so satisfying that you can't help but want them to be true. To make things worse, the media loves these fake stories and spends much more time selling them to a general public audience than they do telling real, compelling stories about the past.

Magical Thinking

Don't you want there to be an Atlantis? I want there to be an Atlantis. Why would a science-minded person want there to be an Atlantis? Because Atlantis is cool! Who wouldn't want there to be a city under the ocean inhabited by Atlanteans with technologies and beliefs beyond anything within our grasp? The world is a more fun place with Atlantis in it. There is only one problem:

Remember the time back in Chapter 2 when I said that science doesn't care about your feelings?

Even though I want there to be an Atlantis, it doesn't mean that I can have it. What is even worse is that there is no evidence at all that Atlantis exists. None. So, according to science we are stuck in a world without undersea cities. Damn! Unfortunately, it is at this point where the media comes in. They play on our wants. They get us to engage in **magical thinking**. Magical thinking is the belief in something that is not supported by any facts. We often engage in magical thinking because we really want something to be true even when the objective world tells us that it is not. The belief that you will earn an "A" grade in class after you got a "C" on the midterm and a "D" on the final is a great example of magical thinking. So is the belief in Atlantis. Here are some classic examples of pseudoarchaeology in the media that are defended using magical thinking:

Atlantis—An island nation that sank under the waves because they went against God. It happens to have been created by Plato in his head—FAKE.

Crystal Skulls—Several found throughout the world, my favorite one was found in Belize in the 1920s. All debunked long ago, and all FAKE.

Shroud of Turin—Claimed to be the shroud of Jesus, but Carbon-14 dating gives it a date of about 1100 AD. This makes it 1,100 years too new and makes it a big FAKE.

Ancient Maya as Ancient Astronauts—The idea that the Maya had rocket technology and blasted off to other worlds. Do I even have to tell you that this is FAKE?

Alignment of the Pyramids at Giza to copy Orion's Belt— Debunked long ago, totally FAKE.

The Sphinx is much older than the surrounding pyramids— The idea that the Sphinx was built long ago (10,000 years or more). Pointless magical thinking—FAKE.

All Pyramids on Earth are related to an ancient Master Culture—No, they're not. Vaguely racist and also FAKE.

Cahokia—A real ancient Native American city on the banks of the Mississippi River in Missouri. At its height at around 1000 AD, it was larger than London at the time. Ten thousand to twenty thousand people lived in this city complete with a 100-foot-tall pyramid. REAL AND AWESOME, but not covered by the media, who would prefer to give us the 1,000th show about Atlantis!

How to Tell a Fake Archaeology Story

How have these obviously false pseudoarchaeology examples lasted for so long? Many of their false stories (especially the ones dealing with aliens) are fabricated using the idea of **diffusion**. Diffusion as it is used in archaeology means that cultural traits begin in one spot and spread over time from one cultural group to another. Diffusion is a real concept in archaeology, and can explain all kinds of historical facts, such as the spread of corn from Central America to Native American groups in the American Southwest and Midwest. More recent inventions diffused throughout the world, such as gunpowder and blue jeans. Where diffusion goes bad is when it is used to explain all major human advancements worldwide, such as trying to tie all major ancient civilizations together under one "super culture." This is called **extreme diffusion**, and this is not scientifically valid or believable using common sense. How you can be fooled into believing this stuff is by using your natural human talent of looking for patterns and similarities in objects.

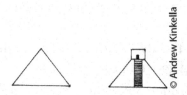

© Andrew Kinkella

Let's make a fake story about how these two pyramids are related. The one on the left is from Egypt, and the one on the right is from the Maya world. Look at the comparison between the outline of these two pyramids. Aren't they similar? They are both triangular, made of stone, and are built to commemorate a powerful ruler. We can use the similarities between these two pyramids to "prove" the connections between them. Since the Egyptian pyramid is several thousand years older than the Maya one, we could say that Egypt was where pyramid building was invented, and then it spread out to all other cultures. The Egyptians could have had boats that made it to the New World. Once there, they taught the Maya how to build pyramids. Or going further out, we can say that aliens made all of them due to their similarities.

This is all utterly untrue. We have never, ever, not once found any piece of Egyptian culture or Egyptian artifact in the New World. Not one artifact. Ever. The true explanation for the Egyptian pyramid and the Maya pyramid is **independent invention**, meaning that both cultures invented a similar thing at different times. If we do ever find Egyptian artifacts in the New World, then that would be real data. Because there is no data, we are able to make up a fake story using extreme diffusion and it will make sense to the general public, which serves to confuse them and make it that much harder to tell the true story of the past.

Dear Archaeology, Please Make a Good Show

Archaeologists often blame shows like *Ancient Aliens* for telling lies to the public and being disingenuous about the facts of history. Although this is true, it is nothing new. When I was a kid, I loved a show called *In Search Of...*, narrated by Leonard Nimoy (Mr. Spock from Star Trek). This show was the 1980s version of *Ancient Aliens*. In the 1990s, the show *Unsolved Mysteries* ran many of these same fake stories after they ran out of unsolved murders to talk about. My point here is that *Ancient Aliens* is just the most recent incarnation of a type of show that has been with us for decades.

The reason that these shows are always successful is that the general public is fascinated by archaeology, and this is the best that we give them. There has yet to be a factual archaeology show that is successful with a broad audience, because the right balance of fun, interest, and factual content has yet to be created for archaeology. Other scientific disciplines such as astronomy have fared much better, with shows like the excellent series *Cosmos* bringing factual content, excitement, and fun together in one program. Archaeology needs a show like *Cosmos*, but it has yet to be made. Archaeologists have only themselves to blame for the fact that they have not created a show that grabs the public's imagination.

My Top Ten Favorite Archaeology Movies

Since archaeology has yet to have a quality television series created for itself, I thought I would talk about the next best thing—archaeology at the movies. Listed are my top ten favorites. You might notice that some of these movies are not really about archaeology! I have chosen them because they remind me about something to do with archaeology, such as living with a small group of people for months. Some of these are high-concept and fantastical, some are all about adventure, some are very realistic, but all of them are fun! At very least, make sure you watch *Raiders of the Lost Ark* if you have not. It is a classic!

1. *Raiders of the Lost Ark/Indiana Jones and the Last Crusade*
2. *National Treasure*
3. *Lost City of Z*
4. *The Mummy* (1999)
5. *Stargate*
6. *The English Patient*
7. *Pirates of the Caribbean*
8. *Time Bandits*
9. *Contact*
10. *Almost Famous*

Honorable Mentions:

1. *Tomb Raider*
2. *The Goonies*

CHAPTER 15

Archaeology and You

The Day I Became an Archaeologist

At what point do you get to classify yourself as an "archaeologist?" In the early days, I could never tell if I was an archaeologist yet or not. Although I was mastering the skillset needed to be an archaeologist, I was working on someone else's project, and I didn't have any advanced degrees. Was I just a student? Was I an apprentice? Was I an archaeologist if my tax returns said I was? Graduate students who were lacking in self-confidence and human kindness would tell me that I was "only a student" and that I was not an archaeologist, even though I was standing in front of them filthy dirty from spending the day excavating at an archaeological site. Although they seemed like jerks, I also felt that they might be partially right. I was never sure I was a full-fledged "archaeologist" until the day I received my membership in the **Register of Professional Archaeologists (RPA)**.

You can only join the RPA if you have completed a master's thesis or have several years of experience in the field. RPA members abide by specific professional conduct and ethical guidelines and are listed on the official register. When I saw my name on the register, I felt like I had finally arrived. Joining the RPA was a big deal for me. It meant that no matter what jerky graduate students said, I was official.

Archaeology and You

We are at the end of this book. Where do you go now? You are left with two choices: To be an archaeologist or to not be an archaeologist. The vast majority of you will pick the second option, and that is understandable! I am not angry at your choice, and I don't feel like I've wasted my time at all, because I have made you into an **Interested Citizen**. Interested Citizens are our great friends in archaeology, because they do things like buy archaeology magazines, watch archaeology programs, and even give money to archaeology projects and preservation groups. They will vote for laws that protect archaeological sites, volunteer at local historical sites, and spread the word about the evils of looting and buying "antiquities." These endeavors are vital for the future of archaeology. If you have chosen path number two, I am happy to have you in the world!

For those of you who have chosen path number one, beware. You have chosen the path of the **Professional Archaeologist**. This path is intrinsically an academic venture, and it is very difficult to be successful in the long term without an advanced degree. Your first step is to start your academic journey.

The pathway toward a career in archaeology has these possible degrees along the way:

> **AA**—Two-year degree (usually takes three). These are increasingly important on your academic journey. If you are at a community college and they offer an AA with an anthropology/archaeology focus, get it! Try to take as many skills-focused classes as possible. This degree can be enough to get you an entry-level job in cultural resource management (CRM) archaeology (especially with skills), but not much more.

> **BA**—Four-year degree (usually takes five). The gold standard "I went to college" degree. Focus in archaeology and anthropology and take as many archaeology skills-focused classes as possible. Also pay attention to your writing skills and get good at them.

At this point, our path diverges. This is where you really need to know what type of job you want within archaeology. Contrary to what most people think, an MA and a PhD do not build upon each other in a ladder fashion. They are two different degrees that serve different purposes. When you are in the post-BA doldrums, you must have an uncommon amount of self-realization and be able to cast yourself correctly.

Which degree is better for you?

MA—Two-year degree (usually takes three). This is often the best degree of all to get for an archaeologist. It separates you from those that have "only" a BA and means that you are a serious professional. If you have a choice, make sure you write a master's thesis instead of merely taking the tests. The thesis will serve as your calling card for later work, and you can mine it later to publish academic articles or use it as an entrée into a PhD program if you realize later that you would like to go onward. The truly smart ones among us will complete an MA degree based on local archaeology and use that to get local CRM jobs!

PhD—Five-year degree (usually takes seven to eight). This is the degree you need if you want to be a college professor or work internationally as the leader of your own project. This choice means that you have to give up a lot of "normal" aspects of life and spend some time as a pure academic/researcher.

I cannot overstate the importance of real **field experience** and attendance at one (but preferably two) **field schools**. It is best to get field experience as soon as possible in the area of the world where you want to work. IMPORTANT NOTE: I also highly recommend getting experience in the local area where you live. As you will see below, your chances of getting an academic job as a college professor are low. You have much better chances getting a job in local CRM archaeology, and you may find it to be ultimately much more fulfilling than a world of academic grant writing. CRM archaeology companies care very little about international field experience—they simply want to see proof that you have worked locally and know the culture history from where you live. As an extra added bonus, it's fun to learn about the deep prehistory of the place where you live!

I have talked about "skills" classes above. The obvious skills classes in archaeology are on-ground field classes in field methods/ excavation, survey and mapping, and laboratory analysis. These are sometimes hard to find academia but be sure to look! If your college does not offer them, but another college in the local area does, see if you can take them at the other place. College credit for these classes does not matter as much as the actual skills that you learn for your career. In addition to these core archaeology skill's classes, there are others that can really help you in your career that are offered outside of anthropology. They include:

Physical Geology and Lab
Earth History
Native American History
Human Anatomy/Zoology
Geographic Information Systems (GIS)
Field Biology
Field Geology
Statistics
Technical Writing
Business
History classes focused on the local history of your area
Computer skills classes, especially in Excel, Access, and
Photoshop/Illustrator.
"Outdoor Education" classes such as hiking, orienteering/
surveying, camping, and scuba diving.

If your institution does not teach the core archaeology skills classes, you can still augment your skillset by taking as many of the above classes as you can find.

The Best Non-Archaeology Classes for Archaeology

Jobs in CRM, the Government, and Academia

Where do you go to find a job in archaeology? Here is a basic jobs breakdown, showing where archaeologists are employed by percentage:

> Academia, including community colleges, universities, and museums—20%
> Government, including federal and state—30%
> CRM firms—50%

The cliché of an "Indiana Jones" type of job at a university, where you teach during the year and work in the field during the summer is rare and requires long years of preparation in the academic world (PhD track) with no guarantees. Government jobs include those in the National and State Parks systems and can be dynamic and rewarding. The largest employer of archaeologists is the CRM world. As described in Chapter 13, CRM is "archaeology for hire" where archaeologists work for firms that make sure developers are adhering to federal and state rules by monitoring their excavations. This is usually where most archaeologists get their first job (this was true for me). One thing is sure—there are many more jobs available in CRM than there are in academia.

Currently, the CRM world is growing, the government sector is stagnant, and the academic world is shrinking. My advice to you is to get as much experience and training as you can to be able to get a job in any of these realms. Keep an open mind and apply to any and all archaeology jobs. Learn and perfect as many relevant skills as you can. The worst thing you can be in the archaeology job world is an academic snob, where you only apply to the rare, four-year university jobs as they slowly and painstakingly become available. In my experience, only a very small handful of academic snobs get jobs, and only after years of their life have been burned away in poverty and post docs. Most academic snobs tend to go nowhere.

Personality Traits of the Successful Archaeologist

If I asked you what personality traits are good for an archaeologist to possess, you would likely tell me traits like patience (for working in the lab), enthusiasm, detail oriented (for making maps and filling out paperwork), and organized. These are all good traits that will help you in archaeology, but the top two most important traits for an archaeologist to possess are **tenacity** and a **sense of humor**.

Tenacity is the ability to see things through, to push forward when things get tough. Tenacity is vital to success in many areas of life. In archaeology, this can mean the ability to physically get up and keep going after a particularly rough day in the field. It can also mean the mental fortitude needed to push onward when you feel lonely, hopeless, and defeated. Tenacity is much more important than intelligence. I know a few archaeologists with PhDs that I would label as "not very smart," but every one of them has tenacity. I also know a few truly brilliant people who went nowhere in their lives because they didn't have the tenacity to push forward when things got tough.

The need for a sense of humor does not mean that you have to constantly make jokes or make light of everything. It is the ability to shrug off setbacks. It is the ability to settle disputes between fellow crewmembers in a lighthearted manner. It is the ability to relax, decompress, and not take things too seriously. A sense of humor enables you to see your spot in the larger world and realize that sometimes archaeology is not the most important thing ever.

Laughing at My Pain: Field Stories from My Life in Archaeology

Throughout my years in the field, I have accumulated many stories about jungle hardships, mishaps, and generally weird events that I have experienced. Below are links to a few classic stories of mine that my students have asked me about over the years. I hope they get you to think about life as an archaeologist in the field. Also, know that I am constantly adding videos to my YouTube channel, and I invite you to check out the latest ones, which will not have QR codes in this book as they will be too new. You are always welcome to leave a comment, and I will do my best to respond. In no particular order, I present to you some stories from the field:

Green Caterpillar of Doom

Stranded in the Jungle in the Afternoon

Guatemalan Bus Ride

One Long Day (my favorite one!)

In the End

I sincerely hope that you have enjoyed this voyage of discovery through archaeology. I hope I have imparted some of my joy of archaeology to you, and that you now understand what archaeologists do during their never-ending search for the story of the past. Archaeology is awesome!

The Archaeology Field Journal

Signature Page

Please fill out the required information, and sign below.

Name: _Mina Allen_

Student ID Number: _____

Major: _Enviornmental Science_

Due Date: _____

I hereby certify that this journal is my own, original work, and agree to abide by all course rules as outlined here and in the course syllabus.

Signature: _____

For The Professor's use only:

Journal Grade _____

Notes:

0

1

2

3

4

5

6

Archaeology Field Journal Grading Rubric

Superior Work

Good Organization

Good Attention to Detail

Excellent Map

Satisfactory Progress

Map Incorrect

Needs More Attention to Detail

Work Suffers from Lack of Effort

Directions Need to be Followed More Precisely

Grammar Problems Detract from Understanding

Needs Better Organization

Bibliography Is Incorrect/Lacking

Excellent Excavation Notes

Nice Lunch Project

Thorough Bibliography

Needs binder

Several Small Errors Throughout

Nice Flake Drawing

Great Six Steps List

Sloppy Printing

Turnitin problems

Excavation Notes and Interpretation Are Lacking

Flake Drawing Needs Labeling

Incomplete/Pieces Missing

Late

Plagiarized

A+	A	A–/B+	B	B–/C+	C	C–/D+	D	D–/F	F
100	95	89	85	79	75	69	65	59	30

INTRODUCTION

Welcome! In the following pages, you will find the outline of the Archaeology Field Journal, your key to success in Introduction to Archaeology. At the moment, this journal is merely an empty framework of projects waiting for you to fill in the blanks. By the end of this semester, it will be a fully realized entity, a reference work, and a memoir of your college experience.

As we progress through the class, you will do these projects to begin to form a skillset in archaeology. I have made these exercises extremely similar to real-world situations in archaeology, so a mastery of these should give you an excellent basis to build upon. Your professor will tell you how they would ultimately like to receive this journal. For me, I prefer that you tear out the finished pages, three-hole-punch them and add them to a slim folder with a binding in the seam or a slim three-ring binder.

Your journal must be your own, solo project. There is no friendly collaboration, sharing, "working together," or otherwise on the material contained in here. This is not to say you cannot work together with your group while you are in class (that is fine, and encouraged!), but the written material MUST BE YOUR OWN. Any overt similarities to anyone else's journal will be considered plagiarism, and you will receive an "F" on this project (and thus, an "F" in the class). The moral here is simple: DON'T CHEAT.

You may want to make scans or xeroxes of your work for safekeeping in case your journal is lost.

And now, onward to Project Number One . . .

ARCHAEOLOGY PROJECT #1:

Draw an Archaeologist!

Draw an archaeologist. This does not take any special artistic talent whatsoever—feel free to use a stick figure as the base of the drawing. What matters here is what your impression is of an archaeologist. What does this person look like? What implements does this person carry or take with them? How do they take these implements with them? How are they dressed? Where are they located? How old are they? Is anyone else with them? Do not be worried about what is right or wrong, and using clichés here is fine. Your *honest impression* of what an archaeologist looks like is what matters.

ARCHAEOLOGY PROJECT #2:

Describe What Attracts You to Archaeology

This is simple. Give me a few sentences about why you are reading this book, or taking an archaeology class, or why you watch archaeology documentaries when they are on TV. Please do not try to impress me! I do not need to hear something lofty like "I am interested in archaeology because I want to collect pure data of the past." What is the REAL reason? I am most impressed with honesty.

I'm taking this class because I needed an "anthropology" credit requirment in order to transfer. I was really excited to see Archaeology as an option though as I've always been intrested in the subject. Most of my knowledge was just from movies and documentaries, not that those aren't fun, but I wanted to know what the subject was actually like. So far this class has been amazing!

ARCHAEOLOGY PROJECT #3:

Translate Archaeological Jargon

You may think that the worst part of archaeology is the bugs or the loneliness. You would be wrong. The worst part of archaeology is archaeological jargon. Your job is to translate the sentences I give you into plain English. I recommend looking up any words you do not understand, and make it make sense to the best of your ability:

1.

2.

Now for extra-added fun, FIND two additional heinously over-jargoned sentences online and print them out here (with your best translation). Look for articles from major offenders like *American Antiquity, Cambridge Archaeological Journal*, or similar. Make sure to cite where they came from.

3.

4.

ARCHAEOLOGY PROJECT #4:

Planning an Archaeological Project

Describe the Six Steps that an archaeologist will follow during the **Process of Archaeological Research**. Name and number each step and describe *in detail* what the archaeologist will do at each point. Be precise and specific and write legibly and carefully. You may use additional sheets if necessary.

1.

2.

3.

4.

5.

6.

ARCHAEOLOGY PROJECT #5

Archaeological Survey

With the initial planning phase of the archaeology project done, it is now time to **survey** and **map** the site. Along with your group, you will make a map of one of the major buildings at Moorpark College. First, your team will choose a datum (a starting point—one of the building's corners). You will then draw a quick sketch map below to orient yourself and to write notes on. After this, you will use a compass to get degree readings from one corner to the next. After you get the degree reading and write it down, you will measure the distance using your pace. Write down the distances. Continue for all four sides of the building. Once all of the corners of the building have degrees and distances, get degrees and distances to one other major feature (large trees, light posts, etc.) from the datum. With this information, you will go home and make a scale map of the area using a   protractor and a ruler. You may use either blank paper or graph paper—lined paper will not be accepted. Interleaf your map into the journal behind this page when you are done.

When writing the points down, you should record them like this (or similar):

1. Datum (corner 1) to corner 2   73 degrees   117 paces

Make sure each point has a number, degree, and distance. Ultimately, you will turn in a map to scale, and a list of points with their degrees and distances. The distances will be converted into meters. We will discuss the specifics of how to make the map in class.

My number of paces for 25 meters is: _____

My "magic number" (the ratio of meters to paces) is: _____

My group number is: _____

SKETCH/NOTES

ARCHAEOLOGY PROJECT #6

Archaeological Excavation

After the survey and mapping of an archaeology site is complete, the initial **excavation** of the site can commence. This time, we will be going outside to do our own archaeological excavation. As a class, we will dig a **1 × 1 meter test pit** (also called a **"unit"** in archaeology). We will experience the initial set-up, excavation, and recording of the test pit. The first objective of this exercise is to foster an appreciation of the skills necessary to engage in the daily practice of archaeology. The second objective is to learn to translate the found artifacts into a plausible story of what happened in the past, based on a very small amount of information that survives into the present.

We will separate into several groups and rotate through so everyone has a chance to help excavate. As we work through this project, you will fill in the form on the next two pages, and then do the interpretation section at home.

My group number is _____

My group was responsible for:

(Space for additional notes):

Site: _____ Unit: _____ Unit Size: _____

Level #: _____ Level (cm): _____ Level volume (m3): _____

Level type: **Screening:**   **Mesh size:**
___arbitrary   ___wet ____dry   ___1/2" ___1/4"
___natural   ___1/8" ___1/16"

Method of excavation: _____

Datum corner: NW, NE, SE, SW

Elevation at start of level (bd or bs): NW:_____ NE:_____
SW:____ SE:____

Disturbance: (1) none (2) bioturbation (3) toots (4) wall fall
(5) vandalism (6) plow zone (7) soil erosion (8) prior construction
(9) Other: _____

Cultural materials present? _____yes _____no

A) Soil Description:

Type	Compaction	Constituents by % (estimate)
sand_____	indurated_____	cobbles_____ loam _____
silt_____	moderate_____	sand_____ clay_____
loam_____	friable_____	silt_____
clay_____		

Comments: (munsell color, texture, compaction, moisture level,
shell or charcoal mottling, etc

_____

_____

_____

_____

B) Evaluation of Degree of Disturbance:

_____

_____

_____

C) Artifacts: (artefact #, description, provenience)

_____

_____

_____

_____

_____

_____

_____

D) Faunal Remains (gross types, condition)

_____

_____

E) Floral Remains (gross types, condition)

_____

_____

F) Provide an *interpretation* of this level based on the descriptions previously listed. Include a discussion, not just a description

_____

_____

_____

_____

_____

_____

Site: _____ Unit: _____ Level: _____

G) Sketch Level Bottom

Scale: _____ cm = _____

Excavator (s): _____ Screener: _____

Crew Supervisor: _____ Date begun _____ completed ____

Site: _____ Unit: _____ Level: _____

ARCHAEOLOGICAL PROJECT #7
Recording Stone Tools

The mapping and excavation of the site is finished; now it is time to put your drawing skills to good use! In the lab, we often spend long hours measuring and drawing artifacts. On the blank paper below, please draw one of the **flakes** from our Stone Tool Extravaganza *to scale*, making sure to label the **platform**, **bulb of percussion**, and any other **attributes** which should also be listed below. You should note artifact attributes such as the type of stone the tool is made from, precise color, specific flaking characteristics (e.g., serrated edge), and give the drawing a scale. *Please draw* **two views**, *one full-face view and one on-edge, and label the attributes on each drawing: and SKETCH.*

SKETCH:

ATTRIBUTES:

ARCHAEOLOGY PROJECT #8

Archaeological Recordation and Interpretation of Your Lunch

With the artifacts now processed in the lab, we must look back to our original research design and begin to **interpret** what happened at the site in the past. For our interpretation project, you will need to begin by eating a lunch. Any lunch is fine, just make sure you have at least three pieces to it (e.g., a sandwich, apple, and drink). Eat your lunch, and then when you are done, get two pieces of blank paper. Choose *one artifact* (leftover container) and make an *exhaustive* list of the attributes (size, shape, material, color, any writing, etc.) of that artifact. Draw the artifact *to scale* on the second piece of paper.

Finally, imagine that 1,000 years has passed. There is an archaeological dig going on in the area where your town used to stand, and the archaeologists have found a feature: It is the remains of your lunch. Using your artifact list and drawing, write a *½ page summary of what the artifact could tell future generations about the past*. This is a chance for you to bring together key themes from the class thus far. All assignments should be typed and double-spaced in 12-point font with one-inch margins. Interleaf your paper in this journal when you are done.

In your short write-up, discuss interpretations you can make using your artifact that may shed light on lifeways from today such as environment, technology, ideology, and/or symbolism, **as long as your statements are based on the attributes of your artifacts**. Look at evidence such as where the food products may have originated, what they may have consisted of, any artwork or designs left on the packages, the construction and materials of the packaging, and so on.

For this paper, do not rely on your ability to read the writing on your artifacts (language could change in 1,000 years!). Instead, rely on an analysis of the artifacts themselves. You may take some artistic license but be sure to write this short paper in a professional manner.

Put the following pieces into this journal in this order, directly following this page:

1. Artifact attribute list (not typed)
2. Artifact drawing
3. Paper (typed—see above)

ARCHAEOLOGY PROJECT #9

Annotated Bibliography

During both the initial research design and final **publication** phase of an archaeological project, references must be studied in order for you to have a thorough background knowledge of both your project area and the other archaeological projects that have come before you. To experience that here, **you will read and analyze one peer-reviewed journal article**. To find one, do the following:

1. Pick any specific topic or theme in archaeology that you find interesting. **Make this the title of your annotated bibliography page**.
2. Look up e-resources on the Moorpark College web or similar.
3. Search for references on your topic on **jstor**—the article you select must be from *American Antiquity, Latin American Antiquity, World Archaeology*, or the *Cambridge Archaeological Journal*.
4. *The article you select MUST be from 1980 or newer, and MUST be at least 8 pages long. Do NOT pick something from a "regular" magazine like National Geographic—it will not count!*
5. Write an annotated bibliography of the reference. First, you must list the reference in correct Society for American Archaeology(SAA) format at the top of the page, just below your title (see below for SAA formatting example). Then, spend one paragraph summarizing the entire article (approx ½ page). Finally, write a second paragraph to discuss how the article specifically addresses your topic (approx ½ page).
6. In sum, your write-up will have a title, a reference (single spaced), and then the two summary paragraphs (double-spaced). Formatting, spacing, and content all count here! It will be about one full page long in total.

This annotated bibliography will be uploaded to Canvas and a copy will also be printed and put into this journal immediately following this page.

SAA Formatting example:
Lucero, Lisa J., and Andrew Kinkella
2015 Pilgrimage to the Edge of the Watery Underworld:
An Ancient Maya Water Temple at Cara Blanca, Belize.
Cambridge Archaeological Journal 25(1):163-185.

Archaeology is Awesome Key Terms and Study Guide

This list of key terms is here to help you study. I recommend writing in the definitions of these terms and concepts as you read the book and watch the YouTube videos. Then you can use this filled-in key terms list as an excellent study guide for any tests that may be coming your way!

PART 1: HISTORY OF ARCHAEOLOGY

CHAPTER 1: INTRODUCING ARCHAEOLOGY

What is Anthropology?
Anthropology
Holism
Cultural Relativism
The Anthropological Perspective

The Four Fields of Anthropology
Cultural
Biological/Physical
Linguistics
Archaeology

What Is Archaeology?

What Does an Archaeologist Do?
Discover
Record
Interpret
   Timeline
Lifeways
Change over time
Protect

What Does the Archaeologist NOT Do?
Looting
Antiquities
Finders' Keepers

Who Is the Archaeologist?
Advanced Degree
Area
Time
Artifact
Skill

Why Bother Doing Archaeology?

People in the Mix
Treasure
Story of the Past

CHAPTER 2: THE HISTORY OF ARCHAEOLOGY: PART 1

Science
Empiricism
Data versus Feelings
Scientific Method
Deductive Approach
Inductive Approach
Law
Theory
Paradigm
Occam's Rule

Early Scientists
Astronomy/Physics—Copernicus/Galileo/Newton
Geology—Hutton/Lyell
    Stratigraphy
    Superposition
    Uniformitarianism
Biology—Darwin
    Natural Selection/Evolution
    Origin of Species 1859
Early Adventurers

Looters—Giovani Belzoni (Egypt)
Explorers—Stephens and Catherwood (Maya)
Antiquarians—Schliemann (Greece)
Thomas Jefferson

The First Modern Archaeologists
General Augustus Lane-Fox Pitt-Rivers (England)
Sir Flinders Petrie (Egypt)
Howard Carter (Egypt) 1922

King Tut

CHAPTER 3: THE HISTORY OF ARCHAEOLOGY: PART 2

The Modern Era (Post WWII)
Reconstruct Culture
Culture
Ritual
Research Question
Theory
Methods

Archaeology Evolves (WW II to Now)
1940s—Dating Revolution
1950s—Universities and Museums
1960s–1970s—Science Rules! (Objective)
    "New Archaeology"
    Experimental Archaeology
1980s–1990s—Humanities Rule! (Subjective)
    Postmodern (Deconstruction)
    Today—Nobody Rules!
    Cognitive Archaeology
Stonehenge

CHAPTER 4: TERMS AND CONTEXT

Ten Key Terms
Artifact/Material Culture
Potsherd
Assemblage

Subassemblage
Feature
Midden
Structure
Mound
Site
Isolate
Culture Area

Context Part 1: What is it?
Matrix
Association
Provenience

Context Part 2: Types of Context
Primary Context
Secondary Context
Taphonomy

Preservation
Constant
Variable

The Ice Man and Pompeii

CHAPTER 5: DATING METHODS

Dating Methods
Measuring Time
Linear
Cyclical
Chronology
Relative Dating
    Stratigraphy
    Seriation
    Three Age System
    Problem—Heirloom Effect
Absolute Dating
    Carbon-14
    Potassium-Argon/Argon-Argon

Dendrochronology
    Old Wood Problem
Others—Thermoluminescence, Obsidian Hydration, Historic Records

History of the Universe
1. Big Bang
2. Formation of Earth
3. Life on Earth
4. Rise of Mammals

The Pleistocene
5. First Human Ancestors/Bipedalism in Africa
6. Out of Africa/The Human Diaspora
7. The Upper Paleolithic Revolution

Tools, Symbolism, Art, Burials
8. Peopling of the New World
9. The Neolithic Revolution

Farming, Cities
10. The Industrial Revolution

The Anthropocene

PART 2: DOING ARCHAEOLOGY

CHAPTER 6: DOING ARCHAEOLOGICAL RESEARCH

The Six Steps:

1. Research Design

2. Set Up

The Archaeology Crew
P.I.
Field Director
Lab Director
Crew
Specialists

3. Field Work

4. Lab Work

5. Interpretation

6. Publication

CHAPTER 7: FINDING A SITE

Mapping
Finding a Site
1. Accidental Discovery
2. Survey
Survey Methods—Sampling

Haphazard
Random
Stratified
Stratified Random
Transect

Survey and Mapping Tools
Datum
Compass
Pace and Compass
GPS
Measuring Tape
String
Transit
Remote Sensing
Ground Penetrating Radar
Pencil and Paper
Recording—Numbering System
Surface Collection

How to Use a Compass

How to Make a Pace and Compass Map

CHAPTER 8: EXCAVATING A SITE

Excavation Types
Auger
STP
Unit/Testpit
1 x 1 Meter
Trench
Salvage Archaeology

Styles of Digging/Digging Process
Horizontal
Vertical
Natural Levels
Arbitrary Levels
Stratigraphy
Sterile
Backfill

Excavation Toolkit
Trowel
Line level
String
Buckets
Shovels
Munsell Soil Chart
Paperwork
Clothing
SHWA

Underwater Archaeology

CHAPTER 9: THE ARCHAEOLOGY LAB

The Archaeology Lab
Organization
Tools—Scales, Bags, Tags, Cameras, Boxes, Shelves, Computers
Attributes = Characteristics
Typology = Category
Categories Based on Characteristics

Chronological
Functional
Stylistic
Material

Material Types
Lithics
Ceramics
Bone
Other—Metal, Glass, Shell, Textiles, Wood, and so on.

Crisis in Curation

Osteology
Sex
Age
Skull:
    Jaw Line
Mastoid Process
Teeth
Brow Ridge
Cranial Sutures
Cranial versus Post-cranial
Pelvis:
    Shape
    Public Symphasis
    Sciatic Notch
Other: Femur, Long Bones

Ceramic potsherds
Sherds
Rim/Body/Base
Plate/Bowl/Jar/Vase/Figurine
Polychrome
Seriation

Stone Tools and Ancient Technology
Lithics
Igneous—Obsidian
Metamorphic
Sedimentary—Chert

Chipped Stone
    Projectile Points—Spear, Atlatl and Dart, Bow and Arrow
    Scrapers, Blades, Flakes
Ground Stone
    Mano and Metate
    Mortar and Pestle
    Jewelry
What Technology Does

PART 3: GREAT THEMES IN ARCHAEOLOGY

CHAPTER 10: THE ENVIRONMENT

The Environment
Paleoenvironmental Reconstruction
Ice Cores
Plants and Animals
Material Culture
    Rock Art
Environmental Fluctuations
Medieval Warm Period
Little Ice Age

Dead Plants
Floral Analysis
Ecofacts
Pollen
Floatation
Light Fraction
Heavy Fraction

Dead Animals
Faunal Analysis
Zooarchaeology
Bones
Coprolites
MNI

Rock Art
Cupules
Pictographs
Petroglyphs
Geoglyphs

Vikings
Easter Island

CHAPTER 11: THE VILLAGE

The Village/Community

The House
Community
House
Housemound
Household Archaeology
Commoners
Activity Areas

The Village
Location
Settlement Patterns
Site Catchment Analysis
Population
Trade
Sourcing
Landscape
Ritual Space

The Chumash Village

CHAPTER 12: THE INDIVIDUAL

The Individual (Part 1)

Data on the Dead
1. Body
2. Associated Artifacts
3. Location and Position

    4. Written Records
    5. Other
Ethics

The Individual (Part 2)

Identity of the Dead
    1. The Facts
    2. Social Ranking/Status/Class
        Elites, Commoners, Definition of Self
    3. Gender (Roles)
    4. Ideas, Beliefs, Religion, Ideology
Ethics

Famous Individuals

CHAPTER 13: THE LAW

The Law
Who Owns the Past?
    1. Antiquities Act
    2. National Historic Preservation Act
SHPO
National Register of Historic Places
Significance
CRM
    Three Phases—Record Search, Testing, Data Recovery
Mitigation
Archaeological Monitor
Dig Bum
OSHA
    3. NAGPRA
    Repatriation
    Native American Monitor
    Kennewick Man

CHAPTER 14: THE FRINGE

The Fringe
Pseudoarchaeology
Wants versus Reality
Good and Bad?
Diffusion
Extreme Diffusion
Independent Invention
Chariots of the Gods
Shroud of Turin, Atlantis, Crystal Skulls

Cahokia

CHAPTER 15: ARCHAEOLOGY AND YOU

Archaeology and You
Interested Citizen
Professional Archaeologist
Field Experience/Field School
Degrees:
    AA
    BA
    MA
    PhD
CRM versus Academia

Jobs in Archaeology
Jobs—Academia, Government, CRM
Money

Top Two Personality Types
Life in Archaeology

Stories from the Field

Bibliography

Kinkella, Andrew

2009 "Draw of the Sacred Water: An Archaeological Survey of the Ancient Maya Settlement at the Cara Blanca Pools, Belize." Unpublished PhD diss., University of California.

2000 "Settlement at the Sacred Pools: Preliminary Archaeological Investigations at the Late Classic Maya Site of Cara Blanca, Belize." Unpublished MA thesis, California State University.

Kinkella, Andrew, and J. Lucero Lisa

2017 "Aktun Ek Nen: Reflections on the Black Mirror Cave at the Cara Blanca Pools, Belize." In *The Archaeology of Underwater Caves*, 182–97, edited by Campbell Peter. Southampton: The Highfield Press.

Kottak, Conrad Phillip

2019 *Mirror for Humanity: A Concise Introduction to Cultural Anthropology*. 12th ed. New York: McGraw-Hill.

Lucero, Lisa J., Fedick Scott, Kinkella Andrew, and Graebner Sean

2004 "Ancient Maya Settlement in the Valley of Peace Area." In *The Ancient Maya of the Belize Valley: Half a Century of Archaeological Research*, 86–102, edited by J. Garber. Gainsville: University Press of Florida.

Lucero, Lisa J., and Kinkella Andrew

2015 "Pilgrimage to the Edge of the Watery Underworld: An Ancient Maya Water Temple at Cara Blanca, Belize." *Cambridge Archaeological Journal* 25, no. (1): 163–85.